A GUIDE FOR BUSINESS LEADERS

WINNING THE WEBSITE WAR

 **4** STEPS TO MARKETING SUCCESS

THOMAS YOUNG

 IND
INTER...

D1280247

ISBN: 194187004X
ISBN 13: 9781941870044
Library of Congress Control Number: 2014954842

Designed by Joni McPherson, mcphersongraphics.com

INDIE BOOKS INTERNATIONAL, LLC
2424 VISTA WAY, SUITE 316
OCEANSIDE, CA 92054
www.indiebooksintl.com

Table of Contents

DEDICATION ix

PART ONE: Introduction

Chapter 1: Book Objective. 1

Chapter 2: What You Will Get from this Book 5

Chapter 3: Four Steps to Web Marketing Success 9

Chapter 4: The Importance of Project
Management and Action Items. 11

PART TWO: The Four Steps

Chapter 5: Introduction to the Four Steps. 15

● **STEP ONE**

Chapter 6: Step One: Strategy 17

Chapter 7: What Business Leaders Must Know
About Web Marketing 23

Chapter 8: What Business Leaders Need to Know
About Google. 27

Chapter 9: Seven Examples of Successful Website
Marketing Strategies. 33

Chapter 10: What is Not a Website Marketing
Strategy?. 37

Chapter 11: How a Website Meets the Needs of
Your Target Market 43

Chapter 12: Website Marketing and Branding 47

Chapter 13: Website Stats and Key Performance
Indicators (KPIs) 51

Chapter 14: Internet and Web Marketing Plan
Outline. 55

Chapter 15: Market Research and User Feedback. 63

Chapter 16: Build a Web Marketing Team 67

Chapter 17: What are the Potential Results from
Successful Web Marketing? 73

● STEP TWO

Chapter 18: Step Two: Website Design and
Development..77

Chapter 19: The Five Elements of Website Design 79

Chapter 20: What Website Visitors Want from
Your Website......................................83

Chapter 21: How to Understand What Website
Visitors Think About..............................87

Chapter 22: How to Meet User Needs by
Understanding Website Usability 91

Chapter 23: How Website Users Get Value from
Website Content...................................95

Chapter 24: Types of Website Content and Usage 99

Chapter 25: Website Taglines 103

Chapter 26: What the Business Leader Needs to
Know About Website Technologies.................109

Chapter 27: How a Website Drives Conversions to
Sales and Leads..................................115

● STEP THREE

Chapter 28: Step Three: Traffic Generation 125

Chapter 29: The Fundamentals of Website Traffic
Generation 127

Chapter 30: How Offline Marketing Contributes to
Online Success 131

Chapter 31: What is Inbound Marketing?..............135

Chapter 32: Push Versus Pull Marketing and
Website Traffic Growth 139

Chapter 33: Everything the Business Leader
Needs to Know About Search Engines..............143

Chapter 34: Understanding Google AdWords and
Other Pay-Per-Click Services.....................147

Chapter 35: The Importance of E-mail Marketing......151

Chapter 36: How "Content Marketing" Drives
Website Traffic and Conversions 155

Chapter 37: How Business Blogs and Content
Drive Traffic..161

Chapter 38: Social Media Strategies for the Business
Leader 165

Chapter 39: Website Partnerships and Links to
Drive Traffic..171

Chapter 40: The Fundamentals of the Mobile Web.....175

● **STEP FOUR**

Chapter 41: Step Four: Monitoring Return on
Investment (ROI) and Tracking Results.............179

Chapter 42: Monitoring Return on Investment
(ROI) in Web Marketing............................181

Chapter 43: What the Business Leader Needs to
Know About Google Analytics......................185

Chapter 44: Web Marketing Stats and Benchmarks 189

Chapter 45: Develop Conversion Strategies to
Drive Growth......................................193

Chapter 46: Conversion Types and Stay-in-Touch
Programs..199

Chapter 47: How to Run a Web Marketing
Meeting...207

Chapter 48: How to Modify Your Web Strategy 211

Chapter 49: Web Marketing ROI Worksheets 215

PART THREE: Implementation and Action Plans

Chapter 50: How to Develop and Assign Work to
Your Web Marketing Team.........................223

Chapter 51: How to Develop Action Plans and
Project Manage Web Marketing....................231

Chapter 52: Web Marketing and the Sales Process.......235

CONCLUSION 244

ONLINE RESOURCES 245

AUTHOR'S BIOGRAPHY 250

PRAISE FOR
WINNING THE WEBSITE WAR

"This book captures the critical issues and the steps any organization needs to take to finally get a website that works."

— Tony Veltri, CEO, Veltri Inc.

"Thomas Young gives all business owners a precious gift: four easy to comprehend steps on how to whip our lazy, underperforming websites into shape. Never again will you have to settle for a mediocre website."

— Henry DeVries, co-author of *How to Close a Deal Like Warren Buffett*

"Thomas's approach is spot on. He has helped us make our websites more relevant to our audience, easier to navigate and much better in terms of look and function. With Tom's assistance we have grown our presence on the web, and it has translated into more revenues. The data covered by Tom in this book is exactly what he did with us to help FitGolf on the web. Thanks, Tom!"

— David Ostrow, CEO, FitGolf

"To have a website that outpaces your competition you need to be two steps ahead! With Thomas's simple Four-Step Process, this book shows you how!"

— Dustin Carreon, CEO, Freelance Electronics

"Since my business opened almost seven years ago, my biggest source of new clients has been the Internet. Tom Young's strategies have taken my web presence to an entirely new level, which has directly improved my bottom line. Winning the Website War is full of creative, productive and effective ideas for getting a bigger slice of the Internet referral pie."

— Lisa S. Jenks, MD, Owner and Medical Director, Genesis MedSpa

"Here's what I like about Winning the Website War: *It's comprehensive. It works as an outline for thinking through a web strategy. Tom's knowledge of the business shows through. Tom's book is a comprehensive overview of all the steps required to build a successful website strategy."*

— Lisa Rogge, Vistage Chair

"Overall, I'm very impressed. Tom's book proved to be genius in timing. I'm agonizing over how to redesign and redevelop my business website. Here's what I find extremely helpful about Winning the Website War:

Organized in short, uniformly structured chapters

Most chapters ended with bulleted action items I can use as a checklist

Readability high with straightforward language, nothing fancy or longwinded

Kept the users' perspective in mind in the explanations of the Four-Step Process

Examples and case studies made the points come to life.

In addition, most of the chapter titles evoke an "I want to know about that" kind of response. They made me eager to dive into the content. Congrats, Tom, on putting your practical and thorough skills into this immensely helpful guide."

— Barbara McNichol, Barbara McNichol Editorial

"Winning the Website War was the answer to our biggest dilemma. We were committed to a traditional marketing strategy that left our company void of sales and an empty pipeline. The changes that seemed obvious were not easily embraced, leaving our company at a standstill. It is when we implemented the four steps that calls started coming in from an unlikely source...our once dormant, newly revitalized website. Thank you for the directional change and this book that has changed our business."

— Steve Fleming, CEO, Alpine Technology Corporation

"This is a great book. It helped me to read about the Four-Step Process while we are transitioning through it. We have followed the Four-Step Process and seen excellent results. I highly recommended this book."

— Jimmy Thompson, CEO, Card Lock Company

"This book gets to the essence of how to win at web marketing. The book reviews the pros and cons of different approaches and provides an action plan to get it right."

— Mikki Williams, CSP, CPAE, Vistage Speaker, Executive Speech Coach

"As a small business that began in the heart of a recession, web marketing was an overwhelming necessity for our company. We followed Tom's Four-Step Process and saw results first hand. This book was THE cornerstone of our online success, without a doubt."

— Travis Turner, Broker/Owner, Turner Associates

"This book helped us understand what really mattered to our website users. The importance of giving your users what they want instead of what you think is best for them cannot be overstated. We all want the fanciest website with the most information about us or our companies, but in some cases that could actually drive your users away. Tom's book really helped Vistage develop a clear strategy for addressing our user base and put us on the path to developing our most successful website yet."

— Andy Ramirez, Vice President of Digital Products, Vistage International

"We are all about systems at our company. I appreciated Tom's Four-Step Process and detailed information to help us capitalize on our Internet marketing efforts. The key business points and Action Items for business leaders will help us focus on the right areas for success. I'm excited to start implementing these strategies today to help us rise above the competition."

— Lain Chappell, CGB, CGR, CAPS, President of Solid Rock Custom Homes

"Thomas Young knows websites better than anyone I know. He has honed his craft of developing, analyzing, and refining websites and online marketing for so many years that his book is only a fraction of what he could share, given enough time and space. Tom brings to this eminently practical book a perspective that goes beyond mere layout and design to understanding the basics of how humans use this highly evolving medium and what it takes to analyze and refine what we throw out there so that it keeps up with real people's interests. Use Tom's book as your guide to this changing world."

— Kent Wilson, Vistage Chair

"If you really want to grow your business from your web site, then Tom's your man. I would highly recommend using the principles in Tom's book or better yet hire Tom. Unless of course, you are my competitor."

— Howard E. Hyden, CEO The Center for Customer Focus

"A great how-to companion for anyone interested in leveraging the internet to grow their business. Tom Young provides a comprehensive yet simple to use four-step approach that will help you win."

— Edgar Papke, Author, *True Alignment*, Vistage International's 2013 Impact Speaker of the Year

"This book is an invaluable reference for some of the tricky situations that come up when you are redoing an underperforming website. This book is a wake-up call for business leaders and the web marketing world. Thomas Young brings up difficult situations, but always with a light touch, that are worthy of examination."

— Karen Meenan, Vistage Chair Colorado Springs

Dedication

Many thanks to all the professionals I have worked with over the past sixteen years in this field. I also have great appreciation for the many clients and their trust in my team and me. I am grateful for the many lessons learned from each client project.

I would also like to thank my Vistage group, with special thanks to my Vistage chair, Kent Wilson, for his guidance and inspiration.

I would like to dedicate this book to my two sons, Bryce and Blake, to my mother Gloria, and to Lori, my wife, for her patience and understanding.

PART ONE:
INTRODUCTION

CHAPTER 1

Book Objective

This book is written for the business leader who wants a successful website. These leaders are fighting the battles needed to launch and manage a winning web marketing program. For the most part they're fighting on two fronts. The first is out-performing their competition and the second is developing an effective web marketing team. The objective of this book is to win at both those challenges.

It is not written for website marketing professionals, although they will get value from this book. It is written for business owners or key managers who are leading web marketing efforts for their companies, but are not going to handle design or technology issues directly. Their job is to make the website productive and provide direction to a team of experts that will be doing the work and following a strategic plan. This book is a starting point for those efforts and presents a proven process for getting results from your website and Internet marketing.

The book is for business leaders at all levels interested in gaining a comprehensive understanding of how to generate leads and grow sales from their online marketing efforts. It is not a technical book, but rather a strategic book that helps business leaders ask the right questions and set a strategic groundwork for web marketing success. Strategy wins wars and the right strategy wins online.

This book is important because many business leaders turn over strategic web marketing efforts and decisions to team members before they take the time to learn the fundamentals and basics of web marketing. Those fundamentals are needed to set direction for this work and to drive results. They are also needed so business leaders can write a web marketing plan and set the right priorities. Lack of web knowledge should no longer be an excuse for the business leader's lack of involvement in strategic online marketing. This book lays the foundation for the involvement necessary to compete online and win the website war.

A Proven Process Gets Results

Smart business leaders and managers know that companies with excellent processes get better results. Yet, most companies fail to follow a proven process or system for marketing on the Internet. They often take advice from people who are not thinking strategically about their business, which leads to poor results. It is also common for web marketing teams to just wing it or to guess at what users want from their website.

This book introduces business leaders to a Four-Step Process for getting results from their web marketing efforts. Your company website and the Internet are critically important marketing resources and can drive success or failure for organizations looking to increase sales, get more leads and retain customers and clients. For these reasons a strategic process is critical to success and just "winging it" will not bring adequate returns on your time and money.

Making the Complex Simple

This book strives to take something that is very complex to most business people and make it simple. Few business leaders have adequate training in the comprehensive nature of web marketing. The Four-Step Process breaks it down into simple and clear sections to help the business leader develop action plans and assign the right people to tasks. This assures the work gets done and you see results from your website. This book is a comprehensive approach to web marketing, and although the focus is primarily on your company website, the book considers social media sites and other web properties that will include content about your company. The book uses the terms "web marketing", "online marketing" and "Internet marketing" to define this comprehensive approach across many online channels.

The chapters in this book can stand alone, but they are best taken together for a thorough and comprehensive experience. Too often business leaders focus on only one part of web marketing and miss the big picture, when it is the comprehensive approach that drives the greatest return. For example, just being found on the first page of Google does not make for a winning web strategy.

Simplifying the world of online marketing into four steps will help business leaders understand the big picture so they can develop a successful strategy. In that way, this book becomes the roadmap and blueprint for a web marketing strategy and Internet marketing plan that can drive results for your business.

Strategies for Every Industry

The strategies in this book are universal and apply across industries and market segments. These best practices for web marketing strategies come from hands-on experience with many types of businesses across many market segments and with a wide variety of websites. The collected recommendations from across market segments is added value to readers as it helps business leaders understand which techniques work across those market segments.

Book Updates

The book will be updated frequently to account for major changes in web marketing. These changes can literally happen overnight, but the key fundamentals will remain unchanged.

Sign up for updates to this book at www.WinningtheWebsite War.com to stay on top of major changes in web marketing that can impact your strategies and keep you ahead of your competition.

TRUE STORY – Only the Names Have Been Changed to Protect Privacy

Kent Bento, the CEO of Bento Leather Products, was in his office when the CFO hurried in. "Have you seen the new monthly sales report for Internet orders?" he asked.

"No," Kent said.

"Well, take a look. Sales are through the roof!" the CFO said.

Bento is a 103-year-old manufacturing company specializing in men's wallets and briefcases with a large and very loyal customer base. However, these loyal fans were not buying from the company website or even finding it in web searches. Keyword research showed that people were looking for the company in much greater numbers than were visiting the website or buying online.

The company's primary strategy was to achieve a higher online conversion rate with an easy-to-use website that featured the products loved by Bento's loyal buyers. The new website was a success and became a key sales channel, attracting not only current customers, but also new buyers who expanded Bento's base of loyal fans.

Here is a summary of what Bento learned from applying the Four-Step Process:

STRATEGY: Target their loyal customer base and identify missing opportunities in their current web marketing strategy to immediately increase sales.

Design and Development: Design and develop an easy-to-use e-commerce website targeting the demographic making up their most loyal customers. Highlight the bestselling products and focus on up-selling new product categories.

Traffic Generation: Build the search engine optimization for their brand name so their website was highly visible in any search for their company name or related searches. Supplement those searches with paid ads through Google AdWords.

Monitoring Return on Investment (ROI) and Tracking Results: The surge in sales resulted in a new marketing focus for the company. Ongoing web marketing meetings and action items are now a major part of the Bento marketing agenda. This is needed to sustain and grow online sales. The team tracks the ROI of every dollar spent on web marketing against online sales.

The Results: Bento reported a 700 percent increase in online sales the first year following implementation of the Four-Step Process. Direct web sales are now a key sales channel for the company.

CHAPTER **2**

What You Will Get from this Book

The strategies and action items in this book will help you grow sales for your company. That is the principle focus of the book and the bottom line. Everything discussed in these pages leads to that end result. You may find that it is impossible to track exactly where the growth comes from because there are many factors working together that drive results. This includes improved website data, a website that is easier to use, and strong, effective website content. This book will show you how to bring together these strategies and more, to drive results and win the battles online against competitors and in finding talent.

If this book has done its job, you will find ways to grow your business from strategic, well-planned and well-executed web marketing. Here are a few things you can expect to get from reading this book:

- Specific action items to *generate leads* and *new sales* from the Internet and web marketing efforts.

- How to implement a *Four-Step Process for driving web marketing* results.

- How to *measure those results* and *determine return on investment (ROI)*.

- How to build a web marketing team to develop and implement action items.

Use the Four-Step Process

This book will drive sales growth from a proven four-step web marketing process. Those processes can be measured for specific ROI, probably better than any other sales or marketing effort performed at your company. You will learn how to prioritize and assign web marketing tasks to the individuals best suited for driving results for each of the four steps.

The only factors that may provide resistance to your achieving your goals will be market forces outside your control and the motivation of the people executing the work. That's not to say you won't have roadblocks along the way, but this book will help you cover the fundamentals and help you rest assured you are doing the right things online to grow your business.

COMMON QUESTIONS

Here are a few common questions we've heard from business leaders that this book will help you answer:

- How do I increase my company sales with web marketing?

- What are my web marketing priorities?

- How do I prepare an effective web marketing plan?

- Who is going to do this work and how do I build a team to get this work done?

- How do I track my return on time and money spent on web marketing?

- How do I know which strategy for marketing my company online will work the best?

- How do I measure success?

- How do I get found on Google and other search engines?

- How can I get inside the head of my website visitors to better meet their needs?

- Is there a process to get results that has worked well for others?

Develop an Action Plan

The recommendations in this book come from more than twenty-five years of marketing experience and it would be a waste of time if they did not translate into action. Most chapters include a list of action items you can complete as part of your web marketing plan which can then be delegated to your team. The book also includes a list of resources and web marketing worksheets that can be used for developing action plans to get results. Your first action item is to read this book and share it with your team!

TRUE STORY – Only the Names Have Been Changed to Protect Privacy

"It is sure nice to see a record sales month, especially after the great year we had last year. This is a very pleasant surprise," said Ralph Moore, sales and marketing director for BC Wire Carts, a leading manufacturer of industrial laundry carts. Their web marketing strategy prior to implementing the Four-Step Process was to have a basic website with a few key products.

"We never thought our website could produce sales at a level worth the investment we would have to make to build a new e-commerce website. Most of our sales come from our distributor network and we did not think customers would want to buy at full retail prices when they can purchase our products at 20 percent less from a distributor," reported Ralph.

As it turns out, customers will pay more to buy direct from the manufacturer on a website they trust with full access to all available products. Distributor websites are often poorly developed and hard to use. Also, coding every product for search engine optimization (SEO) increased traffic 30 percent annually leading to higher sales.

They also tackled a high cart abandonment rate head-on by instituting a cart abandonment e-mail program with excellent results. "If a customer does not complete their shopping cart and purchase, we follow up with an e-mail reminding them about the product of interest. Many of these website users come back and purchase," said Ralph.

The key to success for BC Carts was keeping things simple and focusing on the products. Here are a few things they learned from the Four-Step Process:

Strategy: They designed and developed an easy to use e-commerce website to target buyers of industrial wire carts and baskets. They also included the full complement of products found nowhere else on the Internet.

Design and Development: They allowed website visitors to buy without a login and include all products on the website with their accessories. Up-selling accessories and using shipping incentives to improve conversion rates also helped increase their sales.

Traffic Generation: By coding every product page for SEO, they achieved a page-one ranking in Google for key industry search terms. Hundreds of products were coded for such searches.

Monitoring ROI and Tracking Results: They scheduled monthly web marketing meetings to analyze sales data and make changes as needed to increase sales. Follow-up on all prospective customers who abandoned their shopping carts with a personalized e-mail and description of the products they left in their carts was critical to their success.

The Results: Consistent annual increases in sales and website traffic built the brand and helped grow the company on and off the Internet.

CHAPTER ③

Four Steps to Web Marketing Success

At the core of this book is a Four-Step Process for web marketing results. Each of these four steps is covered in great detail in the following chapters. These four steps are the process business leaders must implement to be successful online and win the website war. Here are the four steps:

1. Strategy

2. Website Design and Development

3. Traffic Generation

4. Monitoring Return on Investment and Tracking Results

Common Sense is Not So Common in Web Marketing

When you first read these four steps you may think they are common sense and that you are already doing them. However, were they common sense before or after you read them? I have found over many years that common sense is not so common in the world of web marketing and the vast majority of companies do not follow these four steps, but rather wing it or take direction from a strong personality on the web marketing team. This is a major reason for the many poorly performing websites you can find on the Internet. In addition, many people get too close to their web marketing work and use a sample size of one approach that can cause your web marketing efforts to miss the mark for many of your targeted segments. Just because you have a preference for how you do things online, does not mean your target market will also approach your online marketing efforts in the same way.

Follow Each Step in Order

The steps should be followed in order, beginning with strategy. Many web marketing mistakes happen because the steps are not followed properly, such as sending traffic to a website with a poor strategy or a site that is hard to use and navigate. Web marketing begins with setting the proper strategy and then executing a website that follows that strategy. After the first two steps are in order, then the focus should be driving traffic. Step four is the ongoing process of tracking results and modifying the strategy to improve results.

The Four Steps Drive Action Items

In this book, the business leader will receive access to deep knowledge on each of these four steps along with specific action items. These action items can be delegated to team members for implementation. In fact, readers will learn how to build a team that will act on each area. This is often a challenge because of the various skill sets needed to be successful in online marketing. The solution is to follow the action items within each step and let the process drive the action items and ongoing work.

Take a look at the four steps again and commit them to memory as you go about your online marketing work.

CHAPTER ④

The Importance of Project Management and Action Items

Web marketing is one area of business and marketing where the best made plans can go haywire and poor project management can lead to major problems. Many of these problems come from the nature of the work and the complexities of online marketing. As you will read in the coming chapters, problems also come from conflicts in the varied skills needed to market online. Project management can become a major obstacle to online marketing results if it is not done well, as it is a key ingredient in winning the website war.

The most common results of poor project management are a delayed website launch, sub-par web stats or poor results as measured in low website conversion rates. Poorly executed project management has resulted in the failure of many website development and marketing projects and the reason why many websites are hard to use or don't make sense. This book provides an outline for very simple methods for website project management and the development of priorities based on the Four-Step Process.

Discipline and Focus

Web marketing project management takes discipline and focus: discipline to track the overall goals of the project and focus to keep in mind the needs of your target market and users of the website. There are many options and various methods for being successful online, but the key is to stay true to your goals of increased sales and better marketing results. A guidepost to help in this area is to focus on decisions that will attract your target market to your web marketing channels and meet user needs. Project managers should keep true to the marketing goals and needs of users. This is easier said than done, but the results are well worth the effort.

Variety of Skills

It takes a project manager with a unique personality to bring together the variety of skill sets that are necessary to implement a website marketing project. Marketing, technology, design and other dissimilar skill sets must come together effectively to get results from web marketing. Project management is the glue that holds this all together.

Many project management challenges happen when one area dominates the others. It is very common for technology staff or designers to set strategic direction for your web marketing efforts. This may not be the best approach. Strategic direction should come from the company's leadership and marketing directors.

The Four Steps and Project Management

Each of the four steps requires different levels of project management. Design, development and traffic generation are much more time intensive and include many more action items. This is where the project manager will spend the majority of time. Step four is almost entirely composed of project management and setting priorities. The four steps help bring purpose and efficiency to the challenges of managing web marketing projects.

Action Plans and Worksheets

This book provides action plans and worksheets that help track your online marketing activities and ensure priorities are set and tasks are completed. The key will be the development of a process following the four steps and hiring the right person to manage the web marketing work. The project manager does not have to be skilled in technology, programming, design or other areas of web marketing. In fact, it is a good idea if the project manager does not have a specific background in any of these areas because that may bring bias into his or her work.

PART TWO:
THE FOUR STEPS

CHAPTER 5

Introduction to the Four Steps

These four steps have been developed over the past fifteen years and are fundamental to website marketing success. The purpose of the four steps is to take the complex area of website marketing, with its many action items and options, and make it more simple and easy to follow. These steps form the foundation for how websites win online battles for market share and attract visitors that convert to sales.

The four steps can also be used as an outline for your web marketing plan. In fact, you will find that going through the Four-Step Process forces you to consider the focus and strategy of your current business and marketing plans in general. This speaks to the value and comprehensive nature of web marketing and how important it is to your company. In fact, your company website is like a business plan that is visible to the world!

Here is an overview and brief description of each step before going into greater detail in coming chapters.

STEP ONE: Strategy

This first step sets the direction for all website marketing efforts. It is important to be clear on the objectives for the website and how conversions take place online. A written strategy that clearly defines the approaches to be taken by your marketing team is best. Strategy answers the all-important questions about why your company is marketing on the web and what you expect to gain. This web marketing strategy is spread across all web marketing channels and may also include offline strategies that coordinate with online marketing.

STEP TWO: Website Design and Development

Step two is the process of designing and developing your website and web presence. This step actually encompasses two areas: graphic design and the technology used to market online. These are combined into one step because they must work together to drive results and are both a tangible expression of your web marketing strategy.

STEP THREE: Traffic Generation

Step three comprises all the activities needed to bring visitors to your website. This step gets a lot of attention and many web marketers put step three at the top of the list of web marketing activities. In reality, there is no need to send traffic to a website until your strategy is well-defined and your website is a clear expression of that strategy. This is also important because driving traffic takes time and money.

STEP FOUR: Monitoring Return on Investment (ROI) and Tracking Results

The final step brings the first three together and is the most important. This involves a process for tracking web marketing results in your web stats and meetings to review web marketing efforts, online conversions and a method for tracking ROI. From this step will come modifications to the web marketing strategies and action plans to improve conversions and drive a strong, measurable ROI. In this step the priorities are set for the team based on clear data and feedback from website users.

SUMMARY

These four steps should become second nature to the business leadership and the web marketing team. It is best to commit them to memory and separate priorities and action items based on each step. Remember to follow these steps in order and to not put the cart before the horse and start driving traffic before you are ready to convert web traffic into customers and prospects. We will now dive deeper into each step and provide you with the tools necessary to succeed in online marketing and winning the website war.

CHAPTER 6

STEP ONE: Strategy

Volumes of books have been written on business and marketing strategy. It is not the goal of this book to discuss the details of how to develop a business strategy or marketing strategy. The focus of this book is on developing a web strategy that most likely involves a translation of your current business success to the Internet or a new web marketing strategy that has the best chance of driving sales results.

It is important to understand how the unique properties of the Internet can be used to develop a web marketing strategy for your company to grow sales revenues. Also, it is very difficult to lead the implementation of a web strategy without understanding the fundamentals of marketing on the web. This book will help you gain that knowledge. Here are a few of the first steps you can take to develop or fine tune your web marketing strategy.

Translate Current Business and Marketing Plans

Most successful businesses have a strong business plan that drives their success. Within this plan will be a sales and marketing plan to drive revenues. The best way to execute a strong web marketing strategy is to translate what works well in your current marketing plan offline to online efforts. Your current marketing plan is the starting point for your web marketing strategy along with an understanding of what has worked in the past offline.

Many businesses have a hard time with this translation to the web. The key is in simplifying what works offline into a few key taglines for your website's home page and navigation system. This will be discussed in more depth and it is the process of defining what you do really well and translating that to your website content that is at the core of your strategy and conversion efforts.

Web Marketing Plan

The process of writing a web marketing plan is an important step toward developing a winning web marketing strategy. It may be necessary to begin writing the plan based on the four steps and watch the strategy evolve as you work through the plan's details. There is great benefit in writing down your strategy and even a one-page written plan is better than no plan at all.

Inside the Head of Website Users

A starting point for developing a web marketing strategy is an understanding of what people want from your online presence and how to meet those needs. The better you can understand the needs of the website users the better you can set a strategy that works. Website users are looking for ease of use, simplicity and convenience. They are looking to have fun and reduce the risks of making a bad decision.

Your website is a representation of your business strategy and a part of what your visitors perceive to be "The Internet." Your website users will have high expectations for your website, just as you do for the sites you visit. Take time and think about why you use the Internet and also take time to understand and get inside the head of your website users. This understanding has a key role in setting a web marketing strategy and in using feedback from your website visitors to modify that strategy.

Research Competitors

The Internet makes the strategies of your competitors fairly transparent. You can see what your competitors are doing and review their websites across industries. As you do this, you will find best practices, along with many worst practices. Take those best practices, modify and improve upon them to improve your own web strategy. In fact, you should research websites across market segments and indirect competitors to find these best practices. Some of the most successful websites often have some of the best online practices and they lead the field. Be cautious of copying websites with a very strong brand and name recognition because they often play by a different set of rules than the typical business website.

Competitive analysis is very important in the early stages of preparing your web marketing plan. Take the time to review other websites and include your observations in your web marketing plan.

18

Keyword Research

Keyword research is the process of determining the phrases and keywords people put into search engines when looking for your products or services. This is essential to search engine optimization (SEO). However, it is also an excellent research method for testing assumptions in web marketing and in preparing your strategy. Researching search results in Google and from other sources is a great insight for your web strategy as a way to understand how people use the web in your market segments. You will find resources for keyword research in later chapters and in the resource section of this book.

Website Taglines

Website taglines are powerful as the most direct and clear translation and communication of your web strategy. Brainstorming tagline ideas and finding ways to simplify your strategy into just eight to twelve words is an excellent exercise to clarify and identify your strategy. Keep in mind that first impressions are very important and website users will only take a few seconds to evaluate the web page they are visiting. Your tagline is the best opportunity to pull them into your website. The taglines on your website should clearly summarize your strategy. Start with a prominent tagline for your home page.

The Conversion Process

Identifying the behavior of visitors to your website and how they will make contact with your company is also a key to developing and defining your strategy. Make a list of how website users will interact or buy from you, and ask questions about how and why they will take steps toward a conversion. Your conversion rate will only be as good as your web marketing strategy.

SUMMARY

Effective online strategy wins, and there is magic in the development of a strategy that gets results and grows your business. All successful companies and marketing plans have this magic. Your challenge is to develop a strategy that can take advantage of the incredible reach and power of the Internet to grow your business. Keep in mind your website may not need a complete redesign, but it may need a strategy update or modification to improve results and win the website war.

ACTION ITEMS

> Meet with key sales and marketing members to brainstorm web strategy approaches.

> Conduct a thorough competitive analysis to find best practices and ways to improve upon your competitors.

> Review your website stats and learn to interpret key business indicators from that data.

> Talk to your customers and conduct simple user-testing sessions to understand how people use your website and what they expect from your site.

> Learn more about the fundamentals of web marketing to develop a smarter strategy.

TRUE STORY – Only the Names Have Been Changed to Protect Privacy

Most real estate agents struggle with online marketing. They usually turn over those responsibilities to their broker agency, such as RE/MAX. This often results in a template website design and very poor quality web marketing. You can't blame them—real estate marketing on the web may be the most competitive industry online. One real estate company broke this mold by following the Four-Step Process and the results speak for themselves.

"The growth we have seen from our new website has changed our company," says Jim Thompson, the founder of Thompson Real Estate. "It has been the best return of any marketing we have done over the years."

The company started as a small father-and-son residential real estate company. After implementing the Four-Step Process in their online marketing, Thompson Real Estate became a major player in their local real estate market in only two years, a real success in a very competitive market saturated with real estate agents and firms.

"We did not have huge expectations when we started working the Four Steps," Jim says. "We expected a well-designed and easy to use website, but the results have exceeded everything we could have hoped for. The website continues to drive new inquiries for us that convert into customers."

Thompson's web marketing secrets include staying disciplined and following the four steps. Their strategy utilizes a website with a highly professional look that rivals any other real estate website on the internet.

"Why not look as big as Zillow or Trulia?" asks Jim. "The consumers want their needs met and our website does that better than any other local real estate company. People call me directly from the website and are surprised that they are actually talking to the owner. They love that level of attention and we respond very quickly to all inquiries."

While many realtors fear the huge national websites, Thompson competes with them head-on. He is also not afraid to invest in web marketing while many of their competitors invest very little.

"We have increased our financial commitment to marketing online significantly and we are happy to do it because of the results we see," said Jim. "Web marketing is paying off because our web marketing plan is based on the Four-Step Process."

Here is what Thompson Real Estate did:

Strategy: Designed their website to look as attractive as the best website in the target market, even though it is a highly competitive market. The site made their company look large and they learned from market leaders.

Design and Development: Leveraged their great looking, professional website to compete on a national level, giving potential clients access to relevant information. This was important because many people move to the Thompson's area from military relocation and other sources.

Traffic Generation: Downplayed the mass market and instead found their niche in online searches, including marketing to prospective customers moving to their city in the near future. They did this by generating content for local neighborhoods in order to capture web searches for those neighborhoods, using AdWords campaigns to target people moving to their town and by providing free access to all home listings in the area.

Monitoring ROI and Tracking Results: Reviewed their website data every month, looking for opportunities to tweak their strategy and make website improvements. The return on their efforts has been phenomenal—they are investing under $20,000 per year in web marketing and seeing a six-figure return.

The Results: The Thompson Real Estate team experienced a significant increase in clients, home listings, closed business deals, and income for the company and its partners. Also, local home buyers and sellers get access to excellent agents they may not have otherwise found.

CHAPTER 7

What Business Leaders Must Know About Web Marketing

The first thing business leaders must know about web marketing is that they are at a significant disadvantage if they do not understand the fundamentals of web marketing. Military leaders can't fight and win battles without knowledge of their weapons, terrain, air space and other factors. This also applies to online marketing.

Business leaders should ultimately be responsible for web marketing success because they drive the strategy for the company and are in the best position to see that their strategy is communicated properly online. They must make sure the website does its job as a branding tool and is on target strategically. Left in the hands of others, this can be a recipe for disaster and a website that misses the mark.

These problems occur when business leaders lack the fundamental knowledge needed to drive web strategy and implementation. Web marketing ignorance is no longer an excuse for not getting involved in online marketing. Doing this can lead to a significant competitive advantage for your company. Many of your competitors will not take the time to learn web marketing fundamentals and will not have the advantage of the Four-Step Process.

This chapter lays out the basics of the business leader's responsibility in understanding web marketing and how to develop an Internet marketing strategy that gets results.

The Basics of Web Marketing

It is critical to understand the fundamentals of web marketing. Here are a few questions you need to be able to answer:

- What are visitors looking to see and read about on our website?
- What type of research do we need to conduct to better know our online visitor?

- How does the website brand our company?
- How is Google important to my business?
- Why is Google the most important search engine and how does it work?
- What are Google AdWords and how do they work?
- What are the keywords people use to find our site in search engines? Why?
- How popular and competitive are those keywords?
- How do visitors convert on our website and become customers?
- How can I use website data as a key performance indicator (KPI) for the company?
- What is the best web development platform for our company? Why?
- How can I build a team to get all this work done?
- How do I measure results?

All the answers and more will be found in the coming chapters of this book.

Strategy Questions

After you learn more about web marketing and develop your web marketing strategies you can ask the following questions:

- What percent of total revenue can be generated from the website and Internet marketing?
- What is the ROI from marketing on the web?
- How does the website brand the business?
- Are we missing opportunities from online marketing?

What is NOT Strategy

You must know what online strategy is and what it is not. Don't listen to team members that are not strategic in their thinking when it comes to your company and business just because they have online marketing experience. Your website strategy should be unique to your company and avoid copying strategies from other websites. Rather, copy best practices that compliment your strategy. This book will help you develop the skills needed to know the difference between poor strategies and strategies to grow sales through online marketing.

The Internet Marketing Plan

Your Internet marketing plan defines the strategy and the key action steps needed to make that strategy a reality. Even a one-page plan is better than nothing! Include a web marketing plan in your overall business and marketing plans. Use the outline in this book to write your Internet marketing plan and set direction for the web marketing team.

Build a Web Marketing Team

Understand the different roles people play in building and marketing a successful website. It is a challenge to build a web marketing team because of the variety of skill levels that must come together to make it work. Also, excellent project management is critical to web marketing. Determine who the leader of this team will be and give them veto power on decision making and final approval. This may be the CEO or business owner.

SUMMARY

Web marketing knowledge is key to setting strategic direction. Business leaders must develop that knowledge to effectively lead their team and set a winning strategy. Don't just settle for what others know and tell you, go and learn about these issues and bring that knowledge back to your web marketing team.

ACTION ITEMS

➤ Just as you read and learn about leading and managing a business, make time to read about web marketing and the Internet.

➤ Subscribe to at least one web marketing e-mail newsletter from the resources section in this book.

➤ Hold regular meetings with your team to review web stats and ask questions about those stats and website results.

CHAPTER 8

What Business Leaders Need to Know About Google

Before we dive deeper into web marketing strategy, let's first review Google. At the time of this writing, Google is the single best resource on the planet for web marketing. Business leaders should have a fundamental understanding of how Google works and what Google is doing on the web. The impact from Google on your web marketing strategy and business in general is significant. Much has been written about Google and here is a summary of what business leaders need to know about one of the world's most successful companies.

Get to Know Google

Google became popular because their home page is so easy to use. They emerged at a time when search engines were very cluttered and not focused on the search on their home page, but rather banner ads. They quickly took advantage of this growth in traffic by introducing online ads through a pay-per-click program called AdWords. This was not a new idea and was already happening at a search engine called GoTo. com, which changed its name to Overture, was eventually purchased by Yahoo and is now owned by Microsoft.

Google surpassed and dominated competitors by providing a very easy-to-use search engine home page that produced excellent search results based on a website's popularity. Google also offered many free tools including Google Analytics for measuring website stats and Gmail. Google's policy of simplicity and giving away free services to grow a huge user base worked very well. Today, more than ever, Google is looking to monetize these services and products into increased revenue from multiple sources.

Google's Popularity

Just about all your customers and prospects use Google. Here are the numbers:

- 80 percent of consumers research on Google before buying.

- 57 percent of business-to-business (B2B) buyers research on Google before contacting a company. This number is higher if you remove government contracting, which has a more structured procurement process that involves less research.

- Google claims a 70 percent search engine market share, but our client statistics show it to be higher.

Your goal is to get found in your target market's research in Google! A basic understanding of how Google works and what they want is critical to making this happen.

What Does Google Want?

A great question to ask is: What does Google want? The better you understand Google's mission, the better you can take advantage of what Google offers. It is important to know that Google has very ambitious goals to be just about everything Internet and more. Here are a few key things to know about Google:

- Google makes it a priority to prevent spam in web searches.

- Google wants to reward websites with great content that is updated on a regular basis.

- Local search and mobile advertisements are a key growth area for Google.

- Facebook and Apple are seen as competitors for Google.

- Google has big plans for Google+.

- They also have ambitious plans for the future of technology (nothing to do with search engines).

- Google is building a significant customer support presence to help people use their many products and build AdWords campaigns.

- Google wants to grow AdWords significantly as most companies are not using AdWords.

- Google gives away many services and products for free and this is likely to change over time as they attempt to recruit new paying customers for AdWords and other services.

- The best web data and statistics collection on the Internet belongs to Google and they are using this wisely to market online.

Google is Branding

Google is now an important part of your branding and marketing plans. Google is so popular that the first page of Google search results is in itself branding for your business. Getting found on the first page of Google for your targeted search terms is not just about getting found, but also about defining your company, services and products. The definition of branding is the impression left in the minds of your target market when exposed to your company. Part of that branding strategy is how your website appears in Google search results.

Sales Prospecting is Now Google Searches

Google has managed to flip the sales process on its head as prospecting is replaced by Google searches. This has driven the growth of "inbound marketing" which we will discuss in more detail in coming chapters. Inbound marketing is the process of bringing people to your website and online content. This pulls them into your company and leads to an interaction which starts the sales process, as opposed to your sales team prospecting or cold calling them for business.

Here are a few questions to ask about how Google is changing your sales process:

- How has Google changed the way your sales team prospects for business?

- Is your sales team finding prospecting more difficult?

- Are you getting found in Google searches for targeted search terms?

- Is your sales team using Google searches to drive sales and leads?

- How does your target market use Google to find your products or services?

Google AdWords

The Google AdWords program is the driving force behind the success of Google. Google ads drive 97 percent of Google's revenue in staggering numbers worldwide. That's currently about $50 billion a year in sales as of 2014. The reason for this huge revenue stream is that the ads work. AdWords has helped thousands of companies grow their sales online.

Most companies are not taking advantage of this marketing opportunity because they do not have the knowledge to run the ads properly or have tried AdWords in the past and did not see results. AdWords is used to drive traffic to your website. As you have now learned, if your entire web marketing process is not effective, then driving more traffic to your site will not bring a return on your time and money.

Google Forces Measurable Value with Google Analytics

Google has forced a lack of measurable value in marketing or advertising to disappear. If your marketing efforts fail to show a measurable return, chances are you will stop funding them. Google has driven this by making everything they do extremely measurable. This is a fundamental shift in marketing, advertising and sales that is still in progress.

Google's major tool to drive this ROI is Google Analytics, a leading website data program run and managed by Google. They give away Analytics for free so you can see for yourself the return and power of web marketing and closely track your AdWords budgets and return. AdWords is also a very solid tracking and monitoring program for website data and online conversions.

Talk to Google on the Phone and with Webmaster Tools

It has historically been very difficult to communicate with Google. It was impossible to reach someone on the phone and hard to know when Google indexes your site and includes it in search results. Google now offers Webmaster Tools, a free tool that allows you to see the communications between your website and Google. Google also has account representatives to help with AdWords setup and questions.

Here is a direct phone number for Google AdWords: 877-906-7955. More to come in later chapters on both AdWords and Webmaster Tools, two must-have Google products to effectively market online.

More Google Tools and Resources

Google is the starting point for the most essential web marketing tools and resources. Google has a variety of tools that are standards in web marketing and statistics. Most of these tools are free, and can be found by searching Google and developing an account with Google under one username and password. Here are a few of the most important Google tools:

- **Google Analytics** — used to measure your website stats in great detail.

- **Google Keyword Tool** — for researching keywords used to find websites.

- **Google Webmaster Tools** — to track how Google has indexed your website in their search engine results and see what search terms are being used to find your site.

- **Google AdWords** — the Google online advertising program.

- **Google Alerts** — Google will track and e-mail content to you as it is posted on the web, based on requested search terms. For example, if you set up an alert for your company name, then any time your company is mentioned on the web Google will send you an e-mail with a link to that new content.

- **Google Insights for Search** — a report showing trends in search by keywords.

- **Google Think Insights** — a newsletter with the latest findings on web marketing and a variety of topics.

In addition to these tools, Google also owns YouTube and Google+ for social media and content distribution.

SUMMARY

It is impossible for the business leader to know everything about Google. The goals are to know how Google can impact your business, understand Google fundamentals and better manage the team driving results for your website on the world's most popular search engine. This knowledge provides a foundation to help you better develop and implement a winning web marketing strategy. In many ways, Google is the current battlefield on which the website war is fought!

ACTION PLAN

> Set up an account with Google to review their tools and resources.

> Keep one master login for your company in a safe place for all Google websites, products and services.

> Read and learn more about Google and their company goals.

> Learn about Google AdWords and how it works.

> Set up Webmaster Tools and submit your website to Google.

> Understand Google's impact on your business based on your alignment with Google's goals and its mission.

CHAPTER 9

Seven Examples of Successful Website Marketing Strategies

Web marketing strategies can certainly be unique to the website of each business. One size does not fit all. There are many examples of website marketing strategies that have proven successful in driving strong ROI. Most of these strategies fall into one of the seven areas below or a combination of these strategies. Here is an overview of each of the seven strategies for successful web marketing. You will learn more in coming chapters.

1. Branding and building trust in target markets

All websites should do this, and for some websites this is the primary marketing strategy. Branding is what your website visitors think about your website and company when they visit the site. It is the power of the first impression and is a strategy in itself. The importance of online branding and the impact your efforts leave on Internet users should be well-defined and present in your web marketing plan and consistent across all web marketing channels. Take time to write down how you will approach online branding and use what has worked offline to support this strategy.

2. Converting website visitors into sales leads

Just about all websites should have a process for converting visitors into prospective customers. This is also a very common strategy and very important, as a majority of people research online before buying in both consumer markets and business-to-business (B2B) markets. There are several steps needed to develop a website that produces leads. An online brochure with basic content will not convert leads at an acceptable conversion rate. Also, there is no need to drive traffic to a website or content page that does not have a strategy for interaction with the user and a path to conversion. This happens best when the conversion process is driven by your overall web marketing strategy.

3. Selling products or services directly online

This is a straightforward e-commerce strategy. If it is possible to sell products online, then your site should have that ability. You will be surprised at what people are willing to buy on the web. Selling directly through your website is the ideal online conversion point.

4. Building a competitive advantage

Make sure your website is the best in your marketplace. Go see what others are doing online and do it better. Keep in mind many of the things that make your site valuable are not expensive. Some strategies to improve your website over a competitor's site are adding written content, photos that tell your story and other value-added items that meet the needs of the website visitors. Content makes a site valuable and is one of your best competitive advantages.

5. Supporting the sales team

Cold calling and other prospecting techniques are more difficult than ever. Salespeople need every advantage they can get to close more sales. A great website that generates leads and provides excellent content is a salesperson's best friend and will grow sales. Website visits can also be used as key benchmarks and steps in the sales process. A website demo of your services and products, a free online audit of your prospective customer's needs, great content and other items can help move prospects more efficiently through your sales process and closer to a closed sale. Your target market has many options and a visit to your website is a key milestone in your sales process.

6. Becoming a thought and content leader

Website content will not only set your site apart and generate more leads, but will also position your company as a thought leader in your marketplace. Many companies and their business leaders are pioneers and leaders in their industry, but their websites fail to support those positions! This is often because the site is lacking a focused content marketing plan. There are many benefits to the development and placement of excellent online content. Google rewards sites with excellent content and visitors become leads based on the content they see and read online. Content marketing will create website results and deserves your attention as a serious web marketing strategy.

7. Building a loyal following

The final strategy involves building followers that allow you to connect with your target market online. This includes building an e-mail list, driving followers in various social media outlets, getting readers to follow the company blog, and more. The Internet and today's world of inbound marketing is perfectly established to build loyal followers in ways that no other marketing channel has been able to accomplish. People can find the companies that suit them best for services, products and information, and companies can easily and very cost effectively market to their followers. This does not happen by chance. It takes solid strategy as well as excellent project management and planning to make this work. This critical strategy will drive leads and sales over the long term.

SUMMARY

Find the right combination of these website marketing strategies to grow your business and increase sales. Be creative and find strategies that are not listed here, but that work for your company. The Internet allows for this creative thinking to prosper, because its reach is unlimited and its scope drives a huge amount of options. These seven fundamental strategies will drive your results.

ACTION PLAN

> Pick a primary website strategy or combination of strategies from the list above.

> Write a web marketing action plan to implement the right strategy and include your approach to the selected strategies in your plan.

> Develop ROI and success indicators to measure the results of each strategy.

> Talk to your sales team and include their input in the website development process to drive leads and complement their sales process.

> Develop a content marketing plan as part of your web marketing plan.

> Develop multiple channels for building a loyal following and start with an e-mail newsletter sign up and monthly content-rich e-mail newsletters.

CHAPTER 10

What is NOT a Website Marketing Strategy?

As you analyze your web marketing strategy and develop your strategic plan it will be easy to confuse some of the things you are currently doing online as strategy, or you may be misled into thinking that these approaches work online. In reality, these mistakes often result in under-performing websites. Here are ten common approaches that often pass for strategy, but do not work.

1. Get something up on the Internet – do it quick and cheap, and we are done.

Many business leaders take the approach of just getting something on the web and that this is better than nothing. However, this strategy can erode your brand and drive potential customers away, to your competitors. A lack of understanding about web marketing should not translate to inaction. Also, getting a website developed at a bargain price generally leads to poor results and can hurt your brand. An expensive website can also crash and burn. It is the right strategy that drives the results. Websites are never done. You may launch a new website, but it is always under construction and should be improved and updated on a regular basis.

2. Everyone else has a website, so we need one too.

Websites are used to define your competitive advantage and communicate clearly what separates your company from the competition. Having a copycat website will not differentiate you or grow your market share. Do not build a website because everyone else is doing it. Build a website to position your company above the competition. Take what is unique to you and your loyal customer base and incorporate that into your web presence.

3. Use the company brochure for the website.

Most brochures do not make good websites. Website visitors will leave quickly if they sense the site's main purpose is to sell or promote. The site's content must have value. Brochure copy is often made up of large blocks of text with interchangeable, marketing-speak content that no one reads. That is the last thing you want on your website. Toss out the company brochure, and look to your website to translate and communicate your marketing strategy in a way that draws people to you online.

4. Our IT or design department handles the website.

Rarely should the IT department or the graphic designers on your team be the leaders of the website marketing strategy. Website marketing strategies must come from the highest levels of marketing. Delegate those tasks to people with strategic marketing and sales experience, or do it yourself. You can learn about the different roles people play in successful website marketing in coming chapters of this book.

5. I haven't been to our site in weeks.

What you give attention to in web marketing drives results. It is always surprising to see how many business leaders have not visited their company websites in some time and do not review their website stats on a regular basis. Chances are, if you are not visiting your website, you see it as dormant and not very important. The work on your company website is never done. Design, development and content updates are an ongoing part of online marketing success. Also, make time to review your website stats, as they are key indicators of marketing and business performance.

6. We don't need a website.

This strategy is very difficult to justify in today's marketing environment, where the majority of buyers research online before contacting a company. This is true in consumer and B2B markets. Every company needs a website.

7. Customers know what we do and understand our website.

Your website should be easy to use and understand. This means that just about anyone who comes to your site will understand what your company does and how you add value. Never assume that people understand your website just because you understand it! This is true of even your most loyal customers. Make it easy for people to refer others to your company from your website. Follow the ten-out-of-ten visitor rule: Ten-out-of-ten visitors that come to your website should be able to easily explain the value you bring to clients and customers. Don't make assumptions about this. Get feedback from your target market and visitors to your website.

8. Our customers don't use the Internet; I don't use it much either.

This is probably a false assumption. Get inside the head of your website's users and you will find ways they can use your website as a resource. A percentage of website visitors will use your website to research your company and that percentage is growing. The question to ask in this case is: How can we take advantage of the Internet to grow our business?

9. We don't have the time or the budget.

This strategy is really an excuse for not doing your homework on web marketing ROI. Website marketing has the best ROI and tracking ability of just about any sales or marketing expense. The best question to ask in this case is: What opportunities are we missing in online marketing?

10. Our sales leads don't come from our website.

Generating leads from a website happens when the web strategy implementation falls in line with the research conducted with the target market. Leads won't come unless you work at it and these leads can be very profitable for your business. These efforts should not happen in a vacuum, but through coordinated efforts with your sales team. Some of your best sales leads may come after they have been referred to your website by your sales team!

SUMMARY

Do these ten approaches sound familiar? Many of them are there by default because business leaders have not taken the time to understand how web marketing can grow their business. Replace these losing strategies with a winning web marketing plan defining how your strategy will win the website war.

ACTION ITEMS

> ➤ Write a website marketing plan and develop a real strategy, following the four steps.

> ➤ Put direction for the website in the hands of marketing and sales strategists at your company.

> ➤ Don't wing it when it comes to web marketing!

> ➤ Your website is an investment and will bring a return if you follow the guidelines in this book.

TRUE STORY – Only the Names Have Been Changed to Protect Privacy

Katie Smith of Schulman Custom Homes was amazed. In her many years selling homes she had never seen this happen before. An out-of-state customer flew into town and walked into the Schulman model home ready to sign a contract for a new home.

"Don't you want to see the floor plan before we start the building contract?" Katie asked.

"Nope," said the customer, "I saw everything I needed on your website and am ready to build a home with your company."

Katie was able to see the results of the Four-Step Process firsthand as the new customer proceeded to buy a $750,000 home based on his Internet research.

"The impact on the Schulman brand has been incredible. Our website strategy is paying off," reported Katie. The strategy involved a closer alignment between target market needs and website design, along with hundreds of online photos highlighting homes built by Schulman.

"Prospective buyers love our website and the photo galleries are very popular. People can view those photos and imagine themselves living in one of our homes," explained Katie. "This has increased inquiries, drastically decreased our bounce rate and increased engagement by visitors."

Custom home builder websites can be hit or miss. Some are well-designed and others are a mess. These sites rarely communicate properly with their target market. The key strategy was to understand the target market for Schulman Custom Homes. Then they were able to more effectively draw those people into the website and eventually into the model home where they could experience Schulman quality. The sales team was able to take over from there.

Here is how Schulman found success with the Four-Step Process:

Strategy: Align the website design and content with the company mission and history so that it matches the needs of their target market.

Design and Development: Design a quality website that matches the company's quality of home building with the online experience of the prospective buyer.

Traffic Generation: Understand that word of mouth is very valuable in building custom homes, and qualified visitors bring a great return. Traffic coming from offline marketing sources is highly valuable.

Monitoring ROI and Tracking Results: Track all leads from the website and follow up with an extensive e-mail marketing program.

The Results: Schulman experienced substantial sales growth and better ROI from sales and marketing expenses. The company no longer exclusively builds model homes for the local Parade of Homes, rather they focus on building relationships with prospective buyers and using their website to solidify and strengthen their brand.

CHAPTER 11

How a Website Meets the Needs of Your Target Market

I f you have had a successful business for any length of time, you have figured out how to meet customer needs. Most successful companies are good at doing this offline, but many are seriously challenged in meeting customer needs through online marketing efforts. The challenge is to translate that success online to grow sales and stay competitive. This, then, is the secret and key ingredient for a successful online marketing strategy for most companies. *Meet customer needs online the same way you meet their needs offline.* This is easier said than done. Here are a few suggestions to help you meet this challenge and better meet customer needs online.

Start With Hot Buttons

Make the time to identify your target market's needs and hot buttons. Talk to your sales team to help you clearly understand how you can help your target market do their job better or improve the quality of their lives. *The good news is your business already does this!* Identify these hot buttons and use them as key benefit statements on your website's home page and throughout the site's content pages. Start with the two or three most important and incorporate that content on your home page. This is what sets you apart and creates key conversion points for website visitors.

Translate What You Already Do Well

Your challenge is to translate to the web what your business does well. Use content on your website to communicate your unique competitive advantage or how you are different and better than other companies in your field. This should be clearly stated in your home page tagline and with photography, graphics and captions. Avoid the temptation to write generic marketing copy. Rather, get into the details of what makes your company stand out and do it briefly and to the point.

Keep it Simple

It's not easy to keep it simple. Web marketing simplicity is strategic and takes discipline. It is also what your website visitors and prospective customers want. Website users are looking for simple and clear content with a call to action. In fact, visitors are more likely to select your company if their evaluation process is made easier when they spend time on your website. They are also more likely to select your company if they feel the process of working with you is easier then working with your competitors. This meets customer needs.

Don't Make Them Think

Users want to get what they need from websites without having to think too much about it. The process should be intuitive and simple. One of the leading books on website usability is actually called *Don't Make Me Think* by Steve Krug, and is highly recommended.

Here are a few guidelines to follow to help website users think less:

- Use few clicks and scrolls on the site.

- Keep the site to three levels deep at the most.

- Make sure users never get lost as they navigate your site.

- Users should not have to leave to another website.

- Use photos, visual elements and scannable text with captions.

- Include easy-to-find contact information and locations.

- Help people solve a problem and improve the quality of their lives.

Web Marketing Research

Talk to your website visitors to confirm their needs and take time to conduct user testing. This can be done cheaply and effectively on the website UserTesting.com. Ultimately, it is hard to meet user needs unless you analyze visitor data, talk to website users and conduct user testing. Remove the guess work and do the research.

SUMMARY

Internet users are online for convenience. They are drawn to
easy-to-use websites that meet their very specific needs. Meeting
those needs are key objectives of your web marketing strategy
and will be at the core of your success online.

ACTION PLAN

> Summarize what your company does well into a tagline of eight
to twelve words and three or four bullet points.

> Place that content on your home page.

> Conduct market research to keep it simple.

> Visit UserTesting.com and learn more about the fundamentals
of website usability and user testing.

> Set up Google Analytics and monitor the data to track website
usage.

CHAPTER 12

Website Marketing and Branding

Online branding is an essential website strategy and is something your website does the minute it begins to attract visitors. In fact, your company website may have no other functionality or purpose than to brand the company on the Internet. How your company is presented online may be the most important piece of marketing, or branding, seen by your target market. This is especially true for those experiencing your brand for the first time online. Let's take a closer look at a few important elements of successful online branding and how to incorporate them into your online marketing strategy.

A Simple Branding Review

There are many misconceptions about branding and a variety of opinions about how to define branding. If you ask ten people "What is branding?" you are likely to get ten different answers! The most basic and simple way to look at branding is to think of it as the answer to this question: *What do people think about our company?* More specifically, what do people think about when they visit your website or social media presence on the Internet? That's online branding and this also translates to what they think about your company.

Website users do not differentiate between your website presence and your offline business. They are one and the same for most website visitors and Internet users. What people think about your website is also branding for your company. This is also carried into your social media presence. This is the power behind strategic web marketing and the reason it should not be taken lightly.

Everything on Your Website is Branding

Everything on your website and in your social media content is branding for your company. Photos, colors, graphics and content seen by the site visitors all form an impression. That impression is branding, and the reason that much thought must be given to your website and online content. Do not add elements to your website just to have them on the website. Every part of your site should have a very specific purpose. Adding unnecessary elements only leads to a cluttered and confusing website, which hurts your brand. People will quickly leave a confusing or cluttered website, and will rarely come back. Visitors make a connection between the branding coming from your website and your ability to deliver services or quality products. Basically, if you have a bad website you are likely to produce bad products and services.

Websites Make a Company Transparent

A website is your business plan on the Internet for the world to see. Companies can no longer hide behind their brand as they did in the past with ads and marketing-based content. Your target market is looking for much more depth and clarity about your company. The company website exposes the business and places the consumer or prospective customer in charge. Consumers are very smart and can see through the company by visiting your website. Be honest and to the point on your site because your company is now transparent.

Your Website is a Silent Brand

Website users leave evidence of their visit which can be found in your web data in Google Analytics, and most will never connect with you directly or provide feedback. They don't make a lot of noise. They are more likely to vote with a click of their mouse and leave your site than to provide feedback on the brand experience. There are a few web stats that are key indicators of a website's general branding experience with users. Total website visits and overall bounce rate are key measurements of your online brand. The bounce rate is a measurement of users leaving your site immediately after only visiting one page, which indicates very little interest.

Declining visits and a high bounce rate are negative brand indicators. Target a bounce rate below 40 percent of all site visitors. Because this happens in a vacuum, if you are not watching your web stats, your brand can deteriorate and you would never know it until you see your sales and revenues drop. This is the power of website branding.

An External Versus Internal Focus

People come to your website with an intention and a strong focus on getting value. They are looking to get information or get something done. The better you can understand user intentions the better you can drive conversions. See your website from your customer's point of view. This is not easy. Most websites are developed from a very strong internal perspective. Avoid the internal biases of your company on your website. This is often seen in website navigation titles and content. Your website must have an external focus to adequately brand your value to visitors.

Photos Can Hurt or Help Your Online Brand

Photos tell a story and users will look at those photos before any other part of the website, especially photos of people. This drives the brand and your key messaging. Unfortunately, most website photos are clip art imagery or stock photos with no captions. Avoid stock photography and use real photos from your company with captions that tell your brand story.

The First Page of Google Results is Branding

Google has changed branding. The first page of Google search results now defines the brand for that search term. Pick the search terms most relevant in describing your company and make sure you show up on the first page of Google. There are many ways to do this and you can read more about it in the traffic generation chapters of this book.

Establish a Voice for Your Brand Online

Content is a key part of online branding. You must have a content strategy and plan for regular content updates and blog posts. Keep in mind that this content must be consistent to avoid brand confusion and come from one central voice or theme for the company. The voice of the brand found in your online content should meet the needs of your target market.

Online Content is Changing Branding

Online content is growing in its use and reach. Telling the story of your company is critical to developing your online brand. If you don't tell your story, people will make one up. This is true whether it is a ten-word tagline or a 1,000-word article. The future of branding online will be very much made up of content.

SUMMARY

Include a clear strategic branding section in your web marketing plan that explains the impression you want to leave in the minds of people that visit your website or social media pages. Review your web stats to confirm your assumptions and measure online branding efforts.

ACTION PLAN

> How are visitors responding to your website?

> Set up and review Google Analytics and get feedback from visitors.

> Work to get the right type of qualified traffic on your website.

> Have a great tagline and photos with captions that communicate your brand.

> Develop an online content strategy and find the team to implement it.

> Research which keywords should cause your website to appear on page one of Google search results.

> Is your website content written from the perspective of your company or your customers? Write in the language of your prospective customers.

CHAPTER 13

Website Stats and Key Performance Indicators (KPIs)

Most business leaders do not track their web stats on a regular basis. This means they are missing out on very important trends that help track overall success for your company. It also means you can gain a competitive advantage by watching your web stats and taking action on what these stats communicate. Your website marketing efforts are important enough that the stats driven by your company's website are KPIs measuring business success. Don't be blind to this. Understand how increasing or decreasing website visits and other web stats impact your company and include that data as a key measurement tool for business success. These data points are the milestones to success in winning the website war.

Get Access to the Data

For most business leaders, the first step is getting access to your website data and reports. Google Analytics is one of the best website statistics programs available. This program is more than adequate for most business websites. All websites should take advantage of this free service. If you haven't done so already, set up Google Analytics. Ask someone on your team to send Google Analytics reports to you on a regular basis, weekly if possible. Also, schedule a monthly web marketing meeting to review these statistics in detail and ask questions.

The Most Important Web Stats

Here are the most important web stats to watch and review with your team:

- Total website visitors

- Number of web pages per visit

- Time on the website and the bounce rate

- Most popular website pages

- Entry pages and exit rates

- Traffic sources, referrers and search engine keywords

- Web goals: conversions and sales tracking

- Shopping cart abandonment rates

- Sales funnels and user paths

There are many more statistics available, but these are a starting point and the most important for monitoring strategic results and KPIs. The data reported in your web stats should be matched against other KPIs in the business. From this comparison, important KPI trends will emerge. One of the most common trends will be the relationship between website visitors and gross revenues. Another trend to review is website engagement and its impact on conversion rates, which also drives gross sales.

As you begin to monitor these stats you will see many comparisons with business KPIs and you can begin to ask questions on how the trends impact each other. The process will also help you find the unique web stats for your business that become KPIs.

Website Stats and Online Conversion Strategies

The most important website key performance indicator is an online conversion. Measuring conversions and how they happen is the key to your web marketing strategy. There are many ways a website visitor can become a customer and many of these paths start with an interaction on your website. All of this data is available in your web stats reports. Determine those conversion points and track them. These are obvious KPIs that have a direct impact on revenue. Here are a few examples of web marketing conversions to track:

- Phone calls or e-mails

- Website submission forms

- E-mail signups

- Blog postings

- Social media following and likes

- Online sales

- Content downloads

- Driving to your store or location

Monthly Web Marketing Meetings

The best place to review website stats, conversions and KPIs are in regularly scheduled web marketing meetings. These meetings become the core of web strategy implementation as they drive the action plans, build accountability and set project completion dates. Here is a typical agenda for a web marketing meeting:

- Web marketing goals and sales targets

- Review of web stats and data

- Website design and development updates

- Traffic generation strategies

- Website content updates

- Social media updates

- E-mail marketing

- Monthly website marketing action plan

Web marketing meetings are reviewed in more detail in upcoming chapters. These meetings are the engines that drive solid KPIs and web marketing ROI.

Extend Website KPIs into the Sales Team Process

Website data and conversions should be tracked as they flow into your sales process and those sales leads begin discussions with your sales team. Make sure your sales team is responding to web inquiries, and track their conversion rate with these leads. This will determine your ROI on web marketing efforts. The better your sales team can convert a web lead, the better the ROI from web marketing. This can all be tracked.

SUMMARY

Web stats are the measurement of the effectiveness of your web marketing strategy. Those stats drive website and business KPIs. They are easily ignored, and it is important that you make an effort to review them on a regular basis. Otherwise, it can lead to poor marketing results without your knowledge or awareness. Website users enjoy their anonymity, but they do leave a trail behind for you to see in your web stats. Tracking that data and working to improve it provide direction for a winning online marketing strategy.

ACTION PLAN

> Set company web marketing targets based on web stats.

> Set up Google Analytics for your website and learn how to read Google Analytics reports.

> Develop a list of the top website marketing KPIs to track.

> Integrate website KPIs into your overall company KPI reports.

> Schedule web marketing meetings and have your team come prepared.

CHAPTER 14

Internet and Web Marketing Plan Outline

A successful web marketing plan starts with the Four-Step Process, understanding your target market, knowing your goals and what you hope to accomplish through online marketing. This plan defines your web marketing strategy and is the blueprint for all web marketing projects including website design and development efforts, traffic generation and conversions. All the elements of your web marketing strategy are included in this plan.

The web marketing plan will answer the following questions:

- How do our online marketing efforts result in sales growth?

- What percent of total revenue can be generated from the website and Internet marketing?

- What is our targeted ROI from marketing on the web?

- How does our website brand the business?

- What opportunities are we missing with our current web marketing?

- What are our specific action items for web strategy, design and development, traffic generation, performance monitoring and ROI?

Web Marketing Plan Outline

Here are the major sections and outline for your web marketing plan by each step in the Four-Step Process.

STEP ONE: Strategy

Strategy — This includes a detailed description of the strategy behind the website and all online marketing efforts. The strategy portion of the plan should answer the following questions:

- What is the purpose of the site?
- What is the branding strategy for the website?
- How will users convert on the website?
- How can the site use simple and clear content with a call to action and a sales funnel to drive conversions?

Website Goals and Objectives — This includes the monthly and annual goals and expected marketing results from the website, such as total visits, leads per month or sales. At a minimum, the following areas should be included in website goals and projections:

- Total website visitors
- Bounce rate
- Search engine traffic
- Referral traffic
- Conversion rate
- Total conversions

Target Market — This section describes the key market segments targeted by the website and their conversion points. This includes the secondary markets in each market segment and their location. Web marketing is very effective at targeting site visitors by location. It should also include a description of the target market's demographics and psychographics. Psychographics is a description of your target market's key characteristics, personality values and related lifestyle variables. This provides direction for the website's taglines, navigation, content, design, usability and more. The objective is to describe the ideal market segment and then develop a website that meets their needs. Include in this section any user behaviors that are unique to your target market. Include market research approaches in this section to help verify your strategy and the needs of your target market.

Competitive Analysis — This section is a thorough analysis of competing websites targeting similar market segments. Include several industry leading websites for best practices. This will also provide many examples of what not to do on your site. This is an essential part of your web marketing plan and most business leaders do not spend enough time reviewing and monitoring competitor websites and strategies. This can help you avoid loss of market share.

Taglines and Content Strategy — The strategy section should include a tagline that is a summary of your company's key value and ties into the strategy for the website. This may include several taglines and strategy for content in general on the website.

Products and Services — Much of the most valuable content on the site will be descriptions of your products and services. Your web marketing plan describes the approaches and organization for this content on your website and throughout the web. Remember to include a strategy for how visitors can buy or inquire about your services or products directly from the website.

STEP TWO: Website Design and Development

Just as commercial or residential building is designed by an architect, so should you develop a blueprint for your website. These are the specific set of instructions turned over to your design and development team as they build the website.

Site Map — This is a critical part of the website design and should be created in your web marketing plan before the site goes to the design phase. The site map is an outline of the navigation structure for the website including the main navigation. The site map can be used to create a wireframe design for the website.

Website Design — Detailed design instructions are included here for the website graphic designer. Design elements are driven by the needs of the target market, not the needs of the designer. This section should include specific instructions and perhaps even a wireframe of the website navigation so your graphic design team can develop an initial home page layout. The following elements should be reviewed in this section.

- Logo design
- Colors and graphic elements
- Photos and images
- Navigation menus
- Secondary navigation and footers
- Fonts and content layout
- Layout recommendations and usability

Website Development — This section is an overview of the various technology platforms for the site selected in part by how many visitors you expect and the site's overall strategy. Ongoing website updates should be considered when selecting a platform along with the amount of outside help versus internal resources needed for site updates. CMS (Content Management System) websites such as WordPress are recommended for the majority of content based websites. This allows anyone on your team to update the website from a browser. This section should define the use of website plugins, forms, e-commerce solutions, integration with current software and other technologies as needed.

Step Three: Traffic Generation

Traffic Generation — Many types of traffic generation action items are included in this section. It includes search engine optimization details, social media, content strategies, search engine advertising and more. Here is a list of the most important traffic generation channels to review in your web marketing plan:

Offline Traffic Generation — This includes all the offline methods used to send visitors to your website. Traffic from this source is usually measured as direct traffic and can be the highest converting traffic of any traffic source.

Search Engines — This includes search engine optimization (SEO), pay-per-click (PPC) advertising, keyword analysis and research and all other efforts to get found in the search engines. Google, Yahoo and MSN comprise almost all the search engines on the web. This part of your web marketing plan outlines how to get found in those search engines for important keyword search terms.

E-mail Marketing — A plan for e-mail marketing is included in this section.

Website Referrals — Building links from websites that are frequented by your target market and that can link to your website.

Social Media — This includes your content strategy for Facebook, LinkedIn, Google+, YouTube, Pinterest and other social media websites.

Content Marketing — Your plan for content distribution throughout the web and your use of content on your website and in social media to pull traffic into your website.

Other Traffic Generation — Other suggestions that can result in traffic generation opportunities are included here.

All these traffic generation channels should be measured closely in your web stats and monitored for ROI. Traffic generation is the most expensive of the web marketing steps and you must have a plan in place for measuring return in the form of website conversions.

Step Four: Monitoring ROI and Tracking Results

Website Data and ROI Objectives — This section defines how web data is used and the process for regular website updates and ongoing content generation for the website and other web marketing projects. Monthly web marketing meetings should be included with sample agendas and team member responsibilities. Websites are never finished. They are ongoing sales and marketing channels for your business that never stop working. This is a good section for ROI and conversion worksheets to help track and measure results.

SUMMARY

Keep in mind the web marketing plan should identify your target market's needs and hot buttons. The plan identifies how to help the target market do their job better or improve the quality of their lives. The good news is your business already does this! A strong web marketing plan is a written document that translates to the web what your business already does well and sets strategic direction. A plan that follows the Four-Step Process is complete and thorough. This plan will result in action items and monitoring techniques that just about guarantee online success and help you beat online competitors.

ACTION PLAN

> The Four-Step Process and the outline in this chapter can be used as an outline for a solid web marketing plan. Review them both in detail.

> Write a web marketing plan, even if it is only one page in length, following these guidelines and recommendations.

> Assign responsibilities to team members to execute the plan's action items.

> Make sure to set up a process for tracking progress toward your web marketing goals.

> Review and modify the plan as needed on a regular basis.

True Story—Only the Names Have Been Changed to Protect Privacy

"Our summer camp registrations are at record levels and we know an easier-to-use website has been a huge factor in this increase," reported Gwen Davis, marketing director for Academy Summer Camps. This organization is on its way to a record summer as registrations are up significantly over last year.

"We launched the new website in February and by the end of March registrations were well ahead of last year and on track to set a record for the year," continued Gwen.

Gwen followed the Four-Step Process, starting with a more focused strategy based on the needs of new parents coming to their summer camps website.

"Our previous website was designed by the parent of a summer camper. It was too internally focused and new parents did not know how to use the website to register their child," reported Gwen. "We were losing valuable new customers to other summer camp programs in the area."

The strategy changed to better understand how parents actually use the site to research the camps and register their child. This was best accomplished through user testing, resulting in a much easier-to-use navigation menu and better organized content. This increased online registrations and better met the needs of website visitors.

"Many people hear about us through word of mouth and visit us on Facebook, but they all end up on our website to research our camps and register their kids," explained Gwen. Following the Four-Step Process resulted in a higher-producing website and increased registrations. Here is what they learned:

Strategy: Get inside the head of your target market and understand how they will use your website to research and register. Conduct user testing to get this right, and avoid designing your site from an internal point of view.

Design and Development: Keep the navigation simple and focus on the key content needed for website visitors to better understand your services and products.

Traffic Generation: Make use of social media for word of mouth, content distribution, and to improve search engine placement.

Monitoring ROI and Tracking Results: Include key conversion points in the website's main navigation menu and track conversions from new site visitors.

The Results: Increased conversion rates from a website that better meets the needs of online visitors will drive business growth and increase sales revenues.

CHAPTER 15

Market Research and User Feedback

The Internet has changed marketing. Business leaders should be aware of two of the most profound changes. The first is the ability of marketing staff to collect highly accurate data from your target markets and the second is the ability to accurately measure the impact and return of various web marketing strategies. This was never possible in sales and marketing to this extent prior to the web. Online marketers know more than ever before about their online consumer, thanks to Google Analytics and other web marketing stats. They can also track conversion sources more accurately, along with what is needed to drive sales.

This has led to a tremendous boost in the accuracy of market research. The Internet and your company website now provide unique opportunities to further get inside the head of your targeted markets and understand how they use your website and why they behave the way they do online. Business leaders should have a basic understanding of how to use the Internet and their websites to collect valuable market research data. Here are a few online market research techniques you can use to improve your web marketing results.

User Testing

User testing is a very powerful form of marketing research. It is the process of observing your website visitors perform basic tasks on your website and monitoring their actions and feedback. User testing can vary widely in its scope and depth. It can go from a formal study in a user testing lab with eye tracking and more sophisticated observation methods, to a very simple over-the-shoulder review of a user as they navigate around your website.

There are several steps that must be followed in order to run a successful user testing session and they include the following:

- **Task Selection** — This is the process of determining the actual tasks users will perform in each session. This can include researching services and products or actually completing an online transaction or conversion.

- **User Recruitment** — Here the targeted users are recruited and scheduled.

- **Technology Selection** — The technology used to record the sessions is included in this step. There are many options available to record desktop computer screens.

- **Session Facilitation** — This is the process used to facilitate the actual testing session.

- **Review and Analysis** — This final part of the process is used to determine the changes needed to improve the site's usability and better meet the user's needs. These are the final recommendations that come from observing the user testing sessions.

There are several principles to follow when conducting user testing. Here are a few to keep in mind:

- Recruit a minimum of five to seven users and group them by market segment and other similar attributes. Combining market segments will lead to mixed results. Only five to seven users can provide significant feedback in effective user testing.

- Make sure the facilitator does not help the users complete tasks, even if a user asks for help. Facilitators should listen and only ask questions. Users should be asked to answer their own questions and show the facilitator what they would do on the website to get an answer or solve a problem.

- Ask the users to think out loud as they navigate around the website. Otherwise, most users don't talk and it is hard to know their intentions.

- Always record your sessions so you can watch the user a second time and see what you missed.

- Watch out for user testing subjects that are looking to please you or be nice. It is common for users to blame themselves when they can't complete a task online.

- Encourage the users to be honest, speak their minds and do what they would do in real life situations.

- Don't ask for users to provide their opinion. People will tend to give positive or neutral feedback when asked for their opinion. It is much better to have them attempt a task on the website.

- User testing can be repeated multiple times to test assumptions and to make sure your improvements are getting the results you expected.

- The best user testing results come when the researcher removes possible bias and remains neutral.

User testing works well for a variety of tasks on just about any type of website. Here are a few common tasks that provide great insights in user testing:

- Find information on a service or product you might buy from this company.

- Look for location information and how to contact the company.

- Review a few competitor websites and research their offerings.

- Search for the website in Google.

- Make a purchase on the site directly.

- Complete a form on the website.

- Research the website's content and blog and provide feedback.

- Sign up for an e-mail newsletter.

- How would you describe the site to others?

Review your statistics in Google Analytics and talk with your marketing team to come up with a complete set of tasks that your website users are most likely to complete online.

UserTesting.com

This is a must-visit website for the serious web marketer. This site allows you to recruit users for brief fifteen to twenty minute user testing sessions of your website. The users find your site and follow your instructions to complete assigned tasks. The sessions are recorded so you can see their mouse movements and hear their reactions to your tasks. All this is done at a very affordable price and is a quick and inexpensive method for getting user feedback.

User Surveys and Focus Groups

Surveys and focus groups are two additional market research formats that you might consider. These research methods take more expertise and skill to conduct, and it is recommended that you find a market research company to conduct these types of studies. A strong bias often exists when these types of research methods are conducted internally, which may not produce the most relevant feedback on your online marketing efforts.

SUMMARY

Online market research goes much deeper than simple feedback on your website. It is excellent marketing information about your company's brand, services, products and more. It is also very accurate information because the website becomes a point of interaction that is now universal to your target market. There is less bias involved in how people use websites because the data is real and feedback is immediate. The data and results that come from user testing will help you significantly improve conversion rates from your website and other online marketing channels.

ACTION PLAN

➤ Include market research in your web marketing plan to verify and support your strategic approaches online.

➤ Conduct market research with your target market in the form of website user testing.

➤ Make user testing and feedback from your target market an ongoing part of your web marketing work.

➤ Read the book *Don't Make Me Think* by Steve Krug. This is a leading book and a very easy read in the area of website usability and user testing.

CHAPTER 16

Build a Web Marketing Team

Business leaders cannot go it alone when executing a winning web marketing strategy. There are too many skill sets that must come together to make this work and anyone that tells you that he or she has all the skills to get it right will most likely fail. In companies of all sizes, developing a successful web marketing team is one of the greatest battles fought by business leaders. It is key to winning the website war. It also the main reason websites fail.

Marketing Versus Technology Versus Design

Three very distinct disciplines must come together to get results from Internet marketing. Take a look at the graphic below. Can these skill sets be any more different? Marketing is concerned with business growth and sales. Technology teams need to make technology work. Designers are creative and artistic. They are interested in colors, graphics, photos and how things look. Many website problems happen because these three skill sets can't come together to get results. In the center is project management, the key to bringing these three disciplines together and completing the project.

Three unique disciplines must work together in web marketing.

The differences in these three areas can lead to all sorts of conflicts in web marketing work. These three skill sets must be managed by a strong project manager and project lead. In many cases, the project lead is the CEO or business leader!

Many business leaders have been extremely frustrated by this process and in many cases it is the principle reason so many websites are delayed or get poor results. The solutions are to have an excellent project manager on your team, understand the many hats people wear in making a website successful and provide the right leadership and direction in each area.

The Many Hats People Wear in Online Marketing

There are eight different job functions found in successful web marketing teams:

- Internet marketing director/manager

- Internet project manager/coordinator

- Internet marketing specialist

- Website research specialist

- Content writer for the web

- Photography and other media

- Graphic designer

- Technology professional

The titles of these job functions may change, but the skill sets and responsibilities do not. Here are brief job descriptions and a brief summary of their responsibilities:

Internet Marketing Director/Manager — This person is responsible for the overall direction and strategy behind the organization's web marketing efforts. He or she reports to upper management and may be part of the company's senior marketing or management team. The director sets the strategy and prepares a budget for the website. This person should have final say on website marketing and the site's development process. It is important not to make website marketing a democratic process and to provide this director the span of control needed to make decisions quickly and in accordance with an approved budget and strategic plan. The director is also responsible for coordinating all offline marketing activities with online marketing efforts.

Internet Project Manager/Coordinator — This staff member reports to the director and is responsible for coordination of all activities and communications from the web team, handling schedules, action plans, development timeframes, meeting coordination and all aspects of bringing the process of web marketing into a cohesive plan. Project managers see that things get done and this work can make or break your website results and ROI.

Internet Marketing Specialist — This person is responsible for driving traffic to the website through all sources, including search engines, pay-per-click, e-mail marketing, affiliates, ads, link exchanges, offline marketing and all other functions that drive traffic to the site.

Website Research Specialist — Gathering feedback from users, web stats and analyzing that data, online surveys, reporting findings and suggestions to the web marketing team are key tasks of this position. This person should stay on top of web trends and changing technologies that can impact gathering data and function as the lead on web marketing research programs. The website research specialist should report on a regular basis to the web marketing team and work closely with the design and development teams to ensure the site is usable and generating conversions. In some cases, this position may be combined with the Internet Marketing Specialist.

Content Writer for the Web — Writing content for your website and e-mail campaigns is the key task of this position. This person must know how to write for the web with content that is scannable and can tell a story with 50 percent fewer words than would normally be used. The person in this role must be able to write scripts for online videos and podcasts. He or she should be able to interview key people in the organization and write effective copy for the web. This is one of the most active positions on the website team and a key part of online marketing success.

Photography and Other Media — This position may actually be a team of people and they are responsible for photos, video, web cams, interactive tours, slide shows, podcasts and all other media presentations of content on the website.

Graphic Designer — This person is tasked with designing the graphic and artistic elements of a website including the logo, navigation systems designs, content placement, photo placement and all other graphic elements on the website.

Technology Professional — The technology position is responsible for the structure of the website and how it operates. This includes the technology platform, hosting, CMS, e-commerce, html, site coding, how updates are made, and all key technology functions. Obviously, the technology person is critical to the website, but should not lead the process. This staff member should take direction and follow the strategy.

External Versus Internal

More than likely, the people at the top of this list are internal to your company. This includes the Internet marketing director and project manager. The marketing and research specialists may also be internal, but will likely need some outside help. Content writers, photographers, videographers, graphic designers and web technology specialists are usually external contractors.

All of these tasks can be handled internally or outsourced, based on the available talent and expected results. Some of these tasks are best outsourced because of the level of expertise needed to run a successful program. This is especially true in the area of search engine marketing. It is also a good idea to outsource tasks where the organization can benefit from the combined experience of a variety people.

Where to Find Resources

The Internet is an excellent resource for web marketing help and there are dozens of excellent websites where you can find help. Most of this work can be done remotely and it is best to find external resources that will respond in a timely manner and are able to connect with your website's strategic vision. Those with a proven track record are your best bet. Set up a phone call and ask for three references. Don't worry if they have specific knowledge in your industry, because that can actually be a hindrance and keep you in a box. Start with a small project and gradually add on work as you see the results.

SUMMARY

These are the key staff functions required to run an effective web marketing program. People will often combine these tasks, which can lead to poor results. The key challenge is to ensure that the right people are handling tasks based on their level of expertise and skills in that area. A common mistake in web marketing is to delegate tasks to individuals who do not have the proper experience, because it is considered a web-related program. The most common example of this is having a technical person responsible for the design of a website or the marketing of the site.

These eight areas are very distinct from one another and should not be merged without careful analysis and a clear division of roles and tasks. Your website is a valuable marketing resource and will need attention each month from this team of specialists.

ACTION PLAN

➤ Determine who the web marketing lead is, and give that lead authority to make decisions on web marketing projects. Avoid web marketing by committee.

➤ Assign a project manager for the entire process to manage the action items.

➤ Determine internal versus external resources and team members.

➤ Find external resources and partners to supplement and enhance the web marketing team, both internally and externally to your company.

CHAPTER 17

What are the Potential Results from Successful Web Marketing?

One of the key goals of this book is to provide the business leader and manager with the information needed to generate results from web marketing efforts. The potential results are determined by your expectations for return on investment (ROI) from sales and marketing efforts. All of the strategies discussed in this book have been developed to drive marketing results and a healthy return on your time and money. Include ROI goals in your web marketing plan and as a target to measure web marketing success.

Start with Proper Expectations

Setting your expectations is the starting point for the web marketing plan and the overall online strategy. Here are a few key questions to ask as you start the process:

- What percent of total revenue can be generated from the website and Internet marketing?

- What is the ROI from marketing on the web?

- How does the website brand the business?

- Are we missing opportunities?

No Quick Fix

There is no quick fix in web marketing, and the return you receive is equal to the work you put in. However, the return is stronger than other forms of marketing. This is true because of the number of people you can reach and the ease with which people can research your company, learn about your products and services and make contact. It is also true because you can track all this activity and determine what works. All of this happens at a very low investment considering the potential return.

The Benefits of Web Marketing

Web marketing offers several key benefits not seen in other forms of sales and marketing. Here are a few potential results you should see from a successful web marketing program:

- Trackable and effective ROI from marketing investments.

- The strongest ROI of any marketing or sales investment.

- A website visitor conversion rate of a minimum of 1 to 2 percent for sales leads.

- A website visitor conversion rate of up to 5 percent for direct online sales.

- The ability to reach an unlimited audience with your message and content.

- A very low-cost method for reaching thousands of people via e-mail marketing.

- The most powerful branding tool for your company.

- The easiest way for people to find you, make contact, and inquire about your services.

SUMMARY

As we conclude the first step in the Four-Step Process (strategy), it is important to keep in mind the end result of your efforts and to set clear expectations. This thought process must be sustained as we go into the remaining three steps of design and development, traffic generation and monitoring ROI and tracking results. There is a lot of work left to be done after you finish setting a clear strategy, and it is important to not get lost in the details and to keep your goals clear as you begin the hard work of implementing your online marketing strategy and making it a reality.

ACTION PLAN

➤ Write a strategic web marketing plan following the outline in this book.

➤ Make sure there is a connection between your goals and your web marketing strategy.

➤ Set very specific conversion rate goals for the website that will drive sales revenues.

➤ Compare online potential results with the cost and potential results of traditional, offline sales and marketing.

➤ Compete the ROI worksheet in this book.

➤ Roll up your sleeves and get to work leading a team that will maximize your return from online marketing and help win the website war.

CHAPTER 18

STEP TWO: Website Design and Development

Step two is perhaps the most involved part of the four steps. This step is the actual design and development of your website. This step can include new websites, redesigned websites and the process of making ongoing design and development updates to your current site to improve results.

This book is not an instructional book for website designers or developers. There are plenty of books for sale covering those subjects. Rather, this book is a strategic overview for business leaders looking to get results from web marketing and beat the competition. For that reason, we are going to focus on better understanding your website visitor as a way of driving improved marketing results and strong ROI.

Think Like Your Website Visitor

One of the best ways to learn how to manage and lead website design and development teams is by understanding website visitors and how to best meet their needs. This will drive conversions, website traffic and business growth. It is the most fundamental step toward a successful website, yet most sites are still developed from the perspective of the designer and developer and not the website user or customer.

The following chapters break down the key elements of website design and development along with clear instructions on how to meet user needs. Find ways to adapt these universal needs to the very specific desires coming from your target market. The better you can accomplish this, the better your website will convert visitors into business.

Thousands of Research Hours on Hundreds of Websites

The approaches and findings you are about to read come from thousands of hours of user testing, user observations and the research and analysis of hundreds of website stats over the past fifteen years. From this work, universal website visitor behaviors and needs have been identified. In other words, this has not just been made up to make a point! You will relate to these recommendations as a user of the Internet and will perhaps think of them as common sense. As stated before, common sense is not so common in the world of web marketing, and many websites builders still ignore these findings and suggestions for improved design and development.

Website Usability a Key Marketing Indicator

This book will introduce a new term to you and the web marketing team that must be a central part of your web marketing effort: usability. This is at the heart of step two (website design and development). How intuitive and easy to use is your company website? We will start by reviewing the five key elements of website design central to usability.

CHAPTER 19

The Five Elements of Website Design

Website design can be overwhelming for many business leaders. It can pull them into the uncharted areas of graphic design and web usability, where emotions rule and what works best is often missed. Business leaders tend to rely on the input of others when it comes to getting this work done. This can lead to negative strategic marketing and usability issues if they miss the mark and do not implement the proper strategic direction. These issues can then lead to an underperforming website.

Understand Design Fundamentals

Business leaders must understand the fundamentals of website design to best lead their company's web marketing efforts. They must know enough to provide direction and to make sure their strategic vision for the website is not lost in the design process. It is a mistake to turn this vision over to graphic design or website development professionals, because they will not understand your vision without your direction. They are most likely to duplicate what they have done on other projects and that may not be the best approach for your website.

Five Areas of Website Design

Here are the five key areas of website design that break down the design process into a more manageable overview and summary. These elements are discussed in more depth in upcoming chapters, and will help simplify what can be a very complex project. Business leaders must be aware of each area and be able to provide direction to their web marketing team in each of these five areas.

1. Navigation and the Site Map

Most website designers don't start with a site map. But they should, as it is a critical part of any website. The site map is the navigation structure for your website that includes all the links, tabs and methods for the site's user to move around the website. *It gets more attention from website visitors than any other website element.* Keep navigation simple and use link titles that are understood by website users. Avoid pull-down menus if possible and only use one main navigation system that is global on all site pages. Your navigation is strategic as well and should be limited to only the most important content pages on your site.

2. Graphic Design

This includes the look and feel of the website and consists of graphics, images, fonts, and other design elements. Design for your target market and not for internal needs or to the preferences of your graphic design team. Many designers will over-design as they work to impress their boss or client. The website design should not get in the way of the site's usability or its ability to communicate the clear value offered by the business. Simple, professional designs get better results. Avoid clutter and any graphics that look like ads, especially as navigational elements. Website users do not click on ads, which make the site appear cluttered. Keep the focus on usability and don't be afraid of white space and fewer links, especially on the home page.

3. Development and Technology

Keep the technology and the website development platform consistent with the website's overall purpose and strategy. Make sure you can control the content on the site and easily make updates from a web browser. The world's most popular website development platform is currently WordPress. It is an open-source, content management system (CMS) that allows your staff to edit content and has no shortage of available developers. Avoid proprietary CMS software programs that lock you into one application and do not allow you to switch providers. Take the time to understand the basics of the technology platform used on your website.

4. Taglines and Website Content

This includes the written content, images, photos and other media on your site. After users scan your photos and use the navigating system, they will quickly rely on the site's content to show them value. Do not take home page taglines for granted, as they are key to the site's success. The home page tagline may be the most important content on the entire website. Make sure it is easy to read and understand. Also, keep it unique to your company. Include a content marketing strategy in your web marketing plan.

5. Market Research and User Feedback

The final area involves getting feedback from your target market and watching your website stats. Think about user testing or surveys to get feedback. Do not ask opinions, but rather ask people to perform a task and do something on the site. You will always learn something new from this feedback and it may surprise you.

SUMMARY

Your web marketing plan should include details from each of these five areas that are in alignment with your strategic plan. This becomes excellent direction for your design and development team to make sure your website performs at the highest levels.

ACTION ITEMS

> Review these five areas with your website designer and developer.

> Determine if the design you are reviewing is appropriate for your target market.

> Make sure you are using a content management system, such as WordPress, for easy content updates.

> Write a navigation plan and site map before you start your design.

> Write an awesome tagline that summarizes your business value in eight to twelve words and is understood by a wide range of website visitors.

> Get feedback from site visitors with user testing and surveys.

> Set up Google Analytics to track website stats.

What Website Visitors Want from Your Website

Earlier chapters reviewed the tactical approaches needed to develop a web marketing strategy and the key elements of website design. Now we are going to go deeper into understanding your website visitors. In fact, we are going to attempt to get inside their heads to better understand their needs and how they will use your website. Let's start with what website visitors want. Web marketing results will only be as good as the team's ability to understand what website users want to accomplish during their visit to your company website.

Understand Your Website Users

A clear understanding of what visitors want from your website is essential when implementing a successful website design or web marketing strategy. This is easier said than done, and most people do not take the time to figure this out. Rather, they do what they *think* or *assume* people want. This "sample-size-of-one" approach can result in a website that does not meet user needs. Design your website from the perspective and needs of your target market, and not of your own.

Business leaders that really understand what website visitors want will drive business growth and marketing results. This is a competitive advantage because most businesses make false assumptions about website user needs and minimize their results. We have worked in the area of user testing and website data analysis for fifteen years and here is what people actually want from websites, based on our data, research and analysis.

Get Information and Solve a Problem

They are not looking to read content about how great your company is and other superlatives. They want very specific information that helps them solve a problem and get information. Your website must help people get this information and help them solve the problem that initiated a visit to your website. This is the most common intent of the website visitor.

Enhance Their Lives and Convenience

The Internet is vastly popular because it makes life more convenient. Your site must do the same. If the Internet were a challenge to use and hard to understand it would not be popular and would be deemed a failure. Yet, many websites are hard to use and understand. Internet users have no problem using Google and finding what they want. For many the struggle begins after they arrive at a website destination. Your website should be easy to use with a depth of content that meets user needs. It should help visitors do their jobs better and otherwise enhance the quality of their lives. It is very easy for people to leave your website and search Google to find other options.

Product and Services Information

Product and services information can sometimes be buried in a website. It should be front and center and very easy to find. The most important factor in driving online conversions and sales is the way users interact with the content about your product and services. A large amount of visits to your product and services web pages is a good sign if you are looking to increase company revenues. Include links to your products and services in your main navigation menu and make this content attractive to visitors. Go into great detail on your product and services. Your product and services landing pages can link to volumes of content. Website users will appreciate this content and search engines will rank your website higher in their search results.

Pricing for Products and Services

Pricing is also very important and should be included when possible on your website. This is true for all types of products and services. Cost is one of the biggest issues on the mind of website visitors and the Internet has driven transparency in pricing. You can price strategically as needed, but your site has to communicate the value that comes with your pricing options and explain how your pricing relates to competitors.

Some companies worry that competitors may see pricing on your website and take advantage of that to hurt your business. For the most part, the upside gain of visitor engagement with your content is more important than competitors having access to this information.

Business Locations and Contact Information

This is very easy information to post on your website and highly useful to website visitors who often come to the site only looking for locations, hours of operation and contact information. All websites should have a Contact Us link in the main navigation and in the website footer. Your mobile website should make this a prominent feature and easy to find in the main navigation.

Delivery and Shipping Information

Shipping and delivery pricing and policies is one of the biggest factors in e-commerce conversion rates. It is important that your website clearly explains how this process works and has fair pricing for shipping. Not including this information will cost you conversions and sales.

Access to Interactive Information, Search and Research

Users expect your website to function like Google, Amazon and other top-of-the-line sites that offer a premium web experience. If you offer any functionality on your site, it must be very good, because it will be compared to the best online resources. This includes everything from a basic search function to advanced e-commerce features. If you have a search option on your website, users will expect it to work as well as Google. Make sure site functionality is part of your strategy and has a purpose, because including it and making it work well can be expensive and time consuming. It is better to not have extra functionality than to have functions that work poorly.

SUMMARY

This may all seem like common sense, but the fact is many websites do not meet visitor needs or drive sales at an acceptable ROI. To win online, you must implement these common sense approaches that are not so common. The better you meet user needs by understanding what visitors want from your website, the better the results of your web marketing efforts.

ACTION ITEMS

> Use the above items as a checklist and verify your site has them covered.

> Check your assumptions about website visitor needs and confirm them with feedback from customers and by reviewing your web stats.

> Make a list of the top ten reasons why people visit your website. Include access to content in each of these areas on your website. If you don't know the top ten reasons, go and ask your target market.

> Question added functionality on your website and only use it when required by your web marketing strategy.

> Make sure products, services and contact pages are on your main navigation.

> Answer the major question: How does your website enhance people's lives and help them do their jobs better?

CHAPTER 21

How to Understand What Website Visitors Think About

The previous chapter reviewed what website visitors want. This chapter will review what website visitors think about as they use the Internet to meet their needs. Getting inside the head of your website visitor helps you better understand their needs and how to build an easy-to-use website that will get results. In our research over the past fifteen years, we have developed a brief list of questions people ask as they visit websites. This comes from thousands of hours spent watching people use the web in user testing sessions and in reviewing the data from Google Analytics for hundreds of client websites.

Here are the questions website visitors ask as they navigate a website. Answer these questions during the website design process to design and build a better website.

What is the website about?

This is the first thought that comes to the website visitor. Ten out of ten people that come to your website should understand what the company does and how it adds value. Not knowing what a site is about in the first five to ten seconds leads to a high bounce rate and low user engagement. People leave websites that they don't understand, or if they are too difficult to figure out how to use. Also, online conversions are almost impossible if the website visitor does not understand the value provided by your company.

What is of value to me?

After the site visitor decides what the site is about, they next ask the most important question dealing with the website's value to them. This happens quickly, and determines if they will stay on the site and dig deeper into the content or leave to find a website that does bring that perceived value. The next step the user will take is to navigate or search the website to help them get to the benefits they are looking for.

How do I navigate or search to find what I want?

The vast majority of web users will go to the navigation menu to start their search. Menu systems that are easy to use and understand are critical to site usability and keeping the visitor on the site. Users will read from left to right on a page, just like they read a book and scan content and navigation links very quickly. They want the links to make total sense to them before they click to see what is on the next page.

What can I do on this website?

The user will search for functionality as a way to meet their needs and get information. Keep in mind that your website must work very well or the user will leave the site quickly. They expect the site to function like Google, Amazon and other popular websites. Functionality must support your web marketing strategy and lead to a conversion or it is probably not necessary.

Is this website safe and can I trust it?

This is a key part of branding and conversions. All aspects of your website must communicate trust, professionalism and safety. A poorly designed website is less trustworthy than a professional site that is easy to use. People want to know if the site will offer value or if it just wants their money. Design a site that builds trust.

Here are a few additional questions on the mind of your website visitors:

- Where am I on the website?
- Should I be somewhere else?
- Where is the company located?
- How do I contact the company?
- Should I tell others about this website?
- How do I buy online?
- How do I contact sales or customer service?
- If I contact them, will they get back with me in a timely manner?

SUMMARY

Understanding what users want from your website and what they are thinking are key starting points and the foundation of your website design and development work. Use this book as a resource to understand the fundamentals of website usability and design to meet user needs. Websites that answer user questions will increase sales and win in competitive online markets.

ACTION ITEMS

> Put yourself inside the head of your website visitors and know the answers to their questions.

> Don't make assumptions about how easy it is for your website users to answer the questions raised in this chapter. Conduct user testing and see for yourself.

> Use these questions in your web marketing plan and to drive design efforts.

> Read the book *Don't Make me Think* by Steve Krug to make your website intuitive so users think less and do more on your site.

CHAPTER 22

How to Meet User Needs by Understanding Website Usability

Business leaders must have at least a basic understanding of website usability in order to lead website design and development efforts. It is important to get out of your own way of thinking about website usability and think like website users. This chapter reviews the fundamentals of how people use websites. These approaches and concepts are often lost in the website design process and it is the responsibility of the person in charge of the process to make sure they are providing leadership and direction in this area.

Website Users Form an Instant Impression

For many in your target market, your website is often the first impression of your company and your brand. First impressions are important online because people have so many options and can leave a website very easily. Also, a first impression is forever and can't be changed.

Website Visitors Begin in the Upper Left Corner

People look at website content the same way they read books and magazines. They start at the upper left corner of the page and their eyes move across the page to the right. The most valuable part of any website page is the upper left corner. This is why the company logo is usually best placed in that position. Many websites have the logo placed in the upper left corner to anchor the site and draw attention to the logo and the company. Use this space wisely and as a best practice, place your logo and tagline in this area of all your web pages.

Photos of People Get Attention

Website users love to look at photos, and pictures of people especially catch their eye. However, many websites use stock photo images and clip art in place of photos of real people. This leaves the user with a low level of value and it is possible to see the same stock photo on multiple websites! Use photos of your team with captions to tell the story of your business. Have professional photos taken for the website and avoid stock photography as much as possible. If you do use stock photography, include a caption or tagline to clarify the message behind the photo. Website visitors will decide on their own what a stock photo's purpose is on your website if you don't clarify its message, and they may get it wrong.

Website Users Ignore Advertisements, Graphics and Clutter

People tend to ignore anything that looks like an online advertisement. Users have been trained to avoid them and stick to content and navigation menus. Website users do not know where they will go when they click on an online ad. These types of graphics are seen as advertising and mostly are avoided. This is reported in web stats and in user testing sessions. Never use graphics, ads or banners for your key calls to action and for website navigation. Put those links in your navigation menu or use well-designed call-to-action buttons that you can track in your stats. Make sure all your graphics, colors and fonts are consistent with the overall design of your website.

Visitors Ignore Marketing Speak Content

Like advertisements, brochure copy and marketing-speak content in large blocks of text are usually ignored by users. This content is usually interchangeable with other websites and actually says very little about your company's value. Here are a few examples of brochure or marketing-speak content:

"Our innovative, state-of-the-art solutions provide our customers with high satisfaction levels."

"Our people make the difference."

"We are committed to the best service and products of any company."

"We provide excellent service, innovative solutions, cutting edge products and top notch support."

Almost any business can make these claims. Avoid marketing-speak brochure copy and keep your content brief and action-focused. Here are examples of content more specific to value:

"Leaders in circuit board design for thirty years and one of the most experienced management teams in the industry. Call us today to find out why Apple, Dell and Cisco come to us for solutions."

Here is a more action-focused approach: "A proven productive tool that saves you 30 percent and improves accounting results. Click here to learn how it works."

Notice a difference? Engage your website users in the same way your leading salespeople engage their prospects, by talking about the real value your company brings to customers.

The Navigation Menu

It is easy to forget about the navigation menu, but it is one of the most important parts of the website's usability. Keep the navigation menu easy to use. Limit it to less than ten main navigation areas and use link titles that are understood by your website users. Keep the navigation consistent on all pages and avoid too many pull-down menus if possible. Top navigation menus work well, but if you need more room put the navigation menu on the left side of the page.

Website Users Scan Content and Move Fast Through the Website

You would be amazed how quickly people scan website content and move around a website. Designers will develop a site thinking that users will take their time and appreciate the design work, photos and content, when in reality, they scan everything in milliseconds looking for something of interest. Use taglines, bullet points and photos with captions to grab the user's attention. Include call-to-action buttons, not ads, and place all your most important links in the navigation menu.

Many Users Leave the Website Quickly

Bounce rates are a key web stat and a best practices KPI measurement of user engagement or lack of engagement. It is not uncommon to see websites with bounce rates over 60 percent. This means that 60 percent of the people that came to the website left immediately without visiting more than one page on the site. Target bounce rates are under 40 percent for lead generation websites and under 30 percent for e-commerce sites. The recommendations in this book will help you lower your bounce rate and reach these targeted levels.

SUMMARY

This chapter is a brief overview of the fundamentals of website usability. This is a critical component of winning the website war. Consider these important guidelines as you build a new website or improve your current site. Focus on simplicity and ease of use to drive high conversion rates, lower bounce rates and increased sales revenues.

ACTION ITEMS

> Design a website that does not make visitors think about how to use the site.

> Make sure there are few clicks and scrolls on each page.

> Keep the navigation to no more than three levels deep.

> Make sure your website users never get lost.

> Keep users on your website so they never have to leave to another website for content or information.

> Use captions on photos and scannable text.

> Include easy-to-find contact information and locations.

> Check your bounce rates and keep them at acceptable levels.

> Write value-added content and remove marketing-speak content.

> Do not use ads or graphics as navigation or call-to-action links.

> Put your logo in the upper left corner of all pages and link the logo to your home page.

> Use photos of real people at your company with captions.

> Talk to your website visitors to confirm their needs.

CHAPTER 23

How Website Users Get Value from Website Content

Content is the fuel that drives the Internet, and in many ways the fuel needed to win at web marketing. Website content is the most important part of your website. It drives conversions, gets you found in search engines, brands your company and much more. Without it there would be very little reason for people to go online and look for value. Content is an important part of both your design and development work and traffic generation. Yet, having excellent content on your website and throughout your web marketing efforts is one of the biggest challenges facing web marketers. This book will help business leaders develop action plans and processes to make sure the right type of online content is found by your target market.

Content comes in many forms and can be defined as anything that is used to communicate with website visitors. Let's dig deeper into website content and how it drives value for your website users. Here are a few questions to ask and guidelines to follow when reviewing website content.

Is it clear what the company does?

The first question to ask involves users understanding what your site is about. A clear ten-to-twelve-word tagline should communicate this so ten out of ten users understand what your company does. Push your web marketing team to make sure the site's message is easily understood and test your assumptions with your target market.

Does the website have a clear branding tagline?

Your tagline should also mention your company's unique value and how you are different from competitors. Take time in preparing your tagline and review the upcoming chapter on tagline writing in this book. This tagline is part of the site visitor's first impression of your company and should be featured on the home page near your logo.

Is the content scannable?

Website users scan online content first and then go deeper to read content of interest. Content should be made up of taglines, headers, bullet points, small blocks of text with links to deeper content pages and other types of easy-to-read content. In fact, your site can have volumes of content for the user to read, but this content should not be on the home page or main landing pages. Volumes of content should be deeper into the website. This is also important to Google, as websites with more content rank higher in Google search results than sites with less content.

Keep in mind it is not easy to read on a computer screen and some content should be easily printable or available in PDF. Also, archive all your blog posts and include newsletter articles on your website. More to come on blog postings in future chapters.

Is the content organized for usability?

The organization of website content is very important, especially as more content pages are added to the site along with a wide breadth of content topics. Make sure your content is easy to find and well organized in your navigation menus. Only use a search function on the site if it's needed, and test it to make sure it produces accurate results. Check your content pages in Google Analytics and set a target of three to four web page visits on average per user session. This is an indicator of well-organized web content. If the average web user visits three or four pages, that person has a high level of interest in your website.

Does the content add value to the user?

This is the most difficult part of website content because value is defined by your website users. Web stats such as number of pages visited, average time on the site at over three minutes, a low bounce rate and other related stats will show you how engaged users are with your website's content. This is the measurement of content value and is directly related to online conversions.

Does the user understand the content?

The content may be written in the language of the user, but it must also be understood by the website visitor. Avoid writing like you speak internally at your company; rather, write in the way a user will understand. This can also be determined in your stats and in user testing.

Is content optimized for the search engines?

Regularly updated content and author authority are the driving forces behind Google's search results. Google will rank higher the sites that have content appropriate for the search results and regular content updates from credible authors. We will go into this in greater depth in the traffic generation and search engine optimization chapters of this book.

Is there a plan in place for content marketing and regular updates?

Content will not write itself and won't get done unless there is a specific plan to make it happen, along with the right people to complete content writing tasks. The use of written content online to support your brand and drive conversions is called "content marketing" and should be included in your web marketing plan. Content marketing is at the heart of a successful web marketing strategy. Once again, we will review content marketing in more detail in coming chapters.

How does the content drive conversions?

Ultimately, this is the final word in website content: does it drive conversions and sales? Picture your website content as a sales funnel that pulls people into contact with your company because of the perceived benefits and value. This is the secret to successful website content. Following the guidelines in this book is a starting point to make sure content delivers on conversions.

SUMMARY

Online content development and content marketing is a large undertaking and requires commitment from many levels in the organization. It is hard work and challenging, but also offers many rewards. In many ways, it is your key to online success. Take the time to learn more about content marketing and determine its importance to your website marketing efforts.

ACTION ITEMS

> Include a content marketing plan in your website marketing strategy.

> Assign content updates to a dedicated web author on the marketing team or outsource it to a writer that can communicate your company story and brand.

> Track the success of your content in your SEO results.

> Develop a content conversion funnel.

> Organize content so it is easy to navigate and scan.

> Write content from the perspective of the website user, not the company.

> Layer your content with brief taglines and bullet points on key landing pages, linking to volumes of content for readers craving more in-depth information.

CHAPTER 24

Types of Website Content and Usage

The Internet offers content in a variety of forms. This gives people the ability to research and learn by their preferred method, whether it be reading, listening to audio, reviewing a slide show, watching a video or other forms of content and media. Millions of people use each of these content types every day on the Internet. Written content is still the most popular form of website content and it can be supplemented nicely by many other forms of content to help communicate the value of your business.

Here are a few examples of content types that you can include on your website:

- Written content
- Video and audio
- Blog postings
- Blog subscription feeds and comments
- E-mail newsletters
- Podcasts (audio and video)
- Webinars or other training
- Informational articles
- Case studies
- Product reviews and testimonials
- E-books and white papers
- PDF files
- Social media postings and comments
- Twitter or micro blog postings

- Press releases (internal and external)
- Slide presentations
- Mobile apps
- About Us pages
- Contact Us pages
- And more...

Here are the channels through which this content can be presented to users:

- Business websites
- Mobile websites
- Website and micro blogs
- E-mail newsletters
- Audio and video
- PDF files
- Social media websites
- Press releases and media websites
- Google docs and other online documents
- Mobile apps
- Branded apps
- Offline marketing
- And more...

Once again, millions of people select the online content channel that is best for them each day. Don't make the mistake of thinking one content channel is best, or that other people do not use a particular channel because you don't use it. Try different content types and channels and measure the results in your web stats.

SUMMARY

The objective of this chapter is to show the business leader the variety of options available for viewing content and distributing online. These content distribution channels form trends and can be unique to your target market. The bullet points above should be part of your content checklist, and each content area should have an action plan and be part of your overall web marketing plan.

For example, mobile devices are one of the fastest growing content segments. Is your website and content optimized for mobile devices? Review your stats on mobile usage and understand how your target market prefers to absorb content online. This is a key to driving web marketing results.

ACTION ITEMS

➤ Determine what content type is most preferred by your target market and make sure you are providing information they value.

➤ Include a content marketing and distribution strategy in your web marketing plan.

➤ Offer content in multiple sources to give website users options.

➤ Distribute this content to other websites that are visited by your target market.

➤ Track and monitor the most popular forms of content and its usage.

➤ Review your content on mobile devices and track mobile stats.

➤ Include visual content with the written word to better communicate value, and always use captions with photos and graphics.

CHAPTER 25

Website Taglines

Writing a catchy tagline may be the most important part of your home page content. The tagline is the sales hook, the most compelling message on your home page and often the starting point in your website's conversion strategy. We have seen the power of website taglines in countless user testing sessions. Not only do taglines summarize the value of your business, they also clearly show users if your website is right for them.

What is a Tagline?

Taglines are eight to twelve word phrases that explain the key benefits of your company. They can be set up as part of your logo, in photo captions, questions, headers, bullet items or other small blocks of text on the site. Taglines are critical because people scan websites, especially first time visitors who are just beginning to understand your company. They can be compared best to newspaper headlines.

Taglines are not slogans or catchy phrases that support the brand, such as Nike's "Just Do It" or Chevrolet's "An American Revolution." These slogans only work when connected to a well-known brand and do not work on their own. However, most small- and medium-sized firms don't have a national brand that is a household name, so their tagline should clarify what the company is about.

Tagline Mistakes

By far the biggest tagline mistake companies make is using a tagline that is generic, cryptic, or not understood by the website visitor. Most users simply overlook meaningless taglines and give them little or no value. Marketers regularly confuse taglines with slogans. Another common mistake is to use internal business speak that is not understood by the website visitors. Many websites do not have a tagline and use a block of text on their home page that users are not able to scan quickly and easily. Others put their taglines into flash or moving text images so that it disappears and makes the user work to read it. Some cluttered sites may have four or five taglines pulling the visitor in several directions, and rotating so that none of them are seen by users.

Examples of Bad Taglines

Here are a few examples of actual taglines and slogans from a few small- to medium-sized businesses. Keep in mind by the time you read this article some of these taglines may have changed, hopefully for the better.

"It's about time. What will you do with yours?" (trustamerica.com)

"Colorado's premier destination resort" (decasino.com)

"Leading IT service and support" (thinkhdi.com)

"Solutions..." (geba.com)

"Where salespeople click and connect instantly" (salesspider.com)

"In Control, In Command" (pcstelcom.com)

"Welcome" (aqua-hot.com)

Let's take a look at each of these taglines and slogans and see if we can get them to make sense and be more effective for website users as they scan the website home page.

Trust Company of America (TCA)
TrustAmerica.com
Tagline: "It's about time. What will you do with yours?"

Many financial services websites use generic taglines that don't usually connect with the visitor or their target market. This company provides service to financial planners that will save them time. A stronger tagline would read:

"We provide the back-end support so you save time."

Questions can also work with taglines:

"Are you wasting time with administrative work?"

These taglines do a much better job of getting at the heart of the issue for financial planners that will hire TCA.

Double Eagle Casino
Decasino.com
Tagline: "Colorado's premier destination resort"

The first major problem here is the Double Eagle is not a resort, but a casino. This is a much better descriptive tagline:

"Cripple Creek Colorado's premier destination casino."

They can also include a differentiator in the tagline like this:

"Cripple Creek Colorado's premier destination casino book online."

"Cripple Creek Colorado's premier destination casino offering hot slots and more."

"Cripple Creek Colorado's premier destination casino with the original Roll the Dice."

HDI
Thinkhdi.com
Tagline: "Leading IT service and support"

Their tagline is generic and thousands of companies could use it. The tagline does not say what they do. Here is a better tagline for HDI:

"Training IT professionals to become excellent at service and support."

Does that clear things up? Of course, we are assuming the user knows what IT means.

GEBA
Geba.com
Tagline: "Solutions…"

The word "solutions" is probably the most commonly used word in taglines on the web. In this case it is the only word in the tagline. In fact, none of the static content on the home page describes what GEBA actually does. A strong tagline will do just that:

"Helping organizations make the right decisions about health insurance and financial security."

PCS
Pcstelcom.com
Tagline: "In Command. In Control"

> This company does not need a slogan because they are not a national brand. What does that tagline mean? PCS provides telephone systems for prisons and are marketing to large prison systems who will purchase and install their phone systems.

> How about this tagline:

> *"A leader in customized, comprehensive telecommunication products and services for prisons."*

> That means more to the user than "In Control. In Command."

Aqua-Hot Heating Systems
Aqua-hot.com
Tagline: "Welcome"

> Another very popular tagline is the word "welcome." This is a left over from the early days of the web. This website uses a block of text on their home page that really needs a tagline.

> Pretty much everything that is said in that block of text can be summed up in this tagline:

> *"Never run out of hot water in your RV."*

Where to Find Great Taglines

A couple areas to see good uses of taglines are newspapers and magazine article headers and photo captions. They have learned the importance of capturing the scanning reader and driving them into content. Also, great marketing companies like Starbucks and Apple make great use of taglines on the Web.

SUMMARY

Make the effort to write a great tagline and don't just wing it. It is the starting point for the website visitor as they begin to engage with your online content. Take a look at your website taglines from the perspective of your website visitors and ask if they make sense. Use the tagline to clarify your company's message and move your website visitors deeper into the site's content. Taglines are the first step to a conversion.

ACTION ITEMS

➤ Follow the instructions in this chapter and write a tagline that sets your company apart and engages website visitors.

➤ Write new taglines that both describe your company and communicate your competitive advantage.

➤ Understand the differences between taglines and slogans and how they are used.

➤ Make sure your tagline is understood by your target market.

➤ Check your bounce rate. High bounce rates on your website may be a sign of a poor tagline.

➤ Connect your tagline with website images and your company logo.

CHAPTER 26

What the Business Leader Needs to Know About Website Technologies

The previous chapters on part two of the Four-Step Process have focused on understanding usability and visitor needs to improve website design. Step two, design and development, also includes website technology and the technical side of how websites are constructed. This book is by no means a technical book, but rather a review of what business leaders should know about web marketing. This essential knowledge includes a basic understanding of the technology behind their company website and how the development process works. This chapter is a summary of that process.

Business Leaders Must Know the Basics and Be Involved

Technology has become a critical part of business and the top leadership in any organization should clearly understand the strategic value of technology for their company. Business leaders can no longer make the excuse of not understanding technology fundamentals or passing it on to others for strategic implementation. Technology is simply too important and today's business leader must be a much more active participant in technology decisions. Poorly- or ill-informed technology decisions within a company can have huge consequences.

The technical side of web marketing is one of these areas. Business leaders do not need to know every detail of website technology, but they do need an understanding of the fundamentals, so they can make better business and budget decisions. Here are a few key points business leaders must know about website marketing technology to better lead web marketing efforts.

Open Source Software Versus Licensed Software

The original business model for software was based on software ownership and the sales of licensed software products. This business model is much less popular as groups of developers collaborate to create free software. This software is called open source software. Developers then make money by selling software extensions or plugins and offering programming support and development services. They can also take the free software and create an application or website that users pay to access.

Most of the software needed to run a successful website marketing program will fall under the umbrella of open source software. This has changed the software industry and the trend continues as younger generations of software users make use of open source software and fewer people pay for licensed software. This has resulted in open source web development software such as WordPress being used as the development platform for a very high percentage of small business websites. It is important to note why this trend is happening and know it is expected to continue.

Content Management Systems (CMS) for Website Development

CMS is a term that is used to refer to software programs used for website development purposes. A CMS website development platform allows anyone to edit the website from any browser with a simple login. This has put web marketing more in the hands of sales and marketing professionals and less in the hands of IT staff.

The current trend in website development is to use open source CMS programs such as WordPress. WordPress is currently the fastest growing and most popular website platform in the world because it is free, open source and easy to use. Most business websites can be built in WordPress at a very affordable cost and those sites will perform very well.

Plugins and Extensions

These are website add-ons that add functionality to a website's performance. All the major CMS website development platforms have hundreds of these plugins available at a relatively small fee. Examples include shipping calculators, form generators, calendars, shopping carts, database management tools and more. It is important to remember that these plugins must be compatible with the most current CMS version running your website and will need regular updates.

110

Templates Versus Unique Designs

There are two approaches to website development in a CMS platform such as WordPress. The first is to build a site with a predesigned template and the second is to convert a unique design into WordPress. Design templates can be purchased for little cost and can make the development process go quickly. However, you're limited to the scope of the plugin and if the template becomes popular, your site may look like other sites using the same plugin. We recommend a unique design for your company based on the strategic vision of your web marketing plan and the needs of your target market.

Technology and e-Commerce Marketing

There are many e-commerce options available and it is a highly competitive market space for software. WordPress does not have an e-commerce system as part of its software, but there are many e-commerce plugins and systems that are compatible with WordPress. This approach is best used when you have minimal e-commerce needs.

High level e-commerce websites should use a dedicated online shopping development platform. These platforms also come in CMS, open source and proprietary systems. When deciding if you should sell online, consider this rule of thumb: If your company can sell products and services online, then you should implement an e-commerce system to develop new revenue streams. You will be surprised at what will sell on the Internet!

Once you make the leap into e-commerce, you must make the commitment to learn all you can about the technology that powers online sales. This is beyond the scope of this book; however, the Four-Step Process and web marketing strategies discussed in these pages are the foundation for online success through e-commerce marketing.

Website Technologies and Multiple Devices

Long gone are the days when the Internet was only available on a desktop computer. There are now dozens of screen sizes, tablets, smart phones and other methods for people to find your website. You must be aware of the percentages of users visiting your website from these varied devices by reviewing Google Analytics data and by visiting your company's website on a variety of popular mobile devices to see what site visitors are experiencing.

Responsive design gives your website the ability to automatically modify each individual web page to the user's screen preferences so web content can be viewed on a variety of screen sizes, and this is an excellent option. You may also consider a mobile website or app for smaller screens and tablets. This is definitely an issue to deal with, and your site should take advantage of the various approaches that allow you to display and update a unique site on a variety of devices from one administrative area.

Web Marketing Reporting

There is a technical component to selecting, tracking and setting up effective web marketing reporting tools. The Internet is loaded with web marketing reporting tools. Whether you are tracking e-mail, social media, content, web leads, web stats or just about any online metric, there is a reporting tool available to track that information. Google continues to be the leader in web marketing reports with Google Analytics, Webmaster Tools and other Google apps. Visit the resources section of this book for more web reporting resources.

SUMMARY

Web-based technologies are the tools used by your team to implement and make your web marketing strategy a reality. An understanding of how these tools are used and the pros and cons of each of the technological options available to business leaders will lead to strategic results. Understanding the basics of technology results in smarter business and marketing decisions. Most IT professionals will recommend what they know best and this may not be the best alternative for your business. Understand technology so you can play an active role in selecting the right tools for your company's online growth.

ACTION ITEMS

> Make time to learn the fundamentals of web marketing technology.

> Build your website in an open source CMS platform, such as WordPress. Evaluate WordPress as an option for your website development platform.

> Do a few Google searches to compare various e-commerce platforms and make sure your IT department brings you the pros and cons of each system.

> Set up Google Analytics, Webmaster Tools and other Google programs as the core of your web reporting.

> Make sure your technology is enhancing your web marketing results and not getting in the way.

> Visit BuiltWith.com to see what technologies are used to build any website and for stats on the most popular website development platforms.

CHAPTER 27

How a Website Drives Conversions to Sales and Leads

In step four of the Four-Step Process we will review ROI and tracking the results of your web marketing efforts. At the core of step four is website conversions. How you design and develop your site will impact its ability to generate online conversions. Let's take a closer look at online conversions as they impact your design and development process. We will go much deeper into this topic when we review step four in later chapters.

The marketing goal of every website should be to convert visitors to customers. This is also the web marketer's great challenge, as many websites are online brochures that focus more on describing the company than converting website users. It starts by developing a conversion strategy that is included in your web marketing plan.

This conversion strategy is the real measure of a website's effectiveness and its ability to convert web users into sales. This is not an easy task and there are no quick fixes. It starts with learning the online conversion process and what works. Converting even a small percentage of your website visitors into sales can drive a very high ROI on web marketing work. Here are several important strategies business leaders should know to effectively drive online conversions.

Develop a Conversion Strategy

It is important to identify how conversions happen by getting inside the heads of the website users and understanding their needs, hot buttons and intent. The better one understands how to meet user needs, the higher the conversion rate. Website users are very focused on getting what they want, and website data is a key indicator of that intent. This can be tracked in your web stats and an online sales funnel, e-commerce data or goal completion. Survey the target market and conduct user testing to better understand user goals and use that information to develop the strategy.

The website should clearly communicate the value and benefits of doing business with your company. Translate to the web what your business does well and use that to drive a conversion strategy.

Define Your Online Conversions

Websites exist for conversions. Yet most websites do not fully take advantage of the variety of conversion options and strategies. Many types of visitor interactions should be measured and are considered conversions. Start the conversion process by clearly identifying the conversions most appropriate for your web marketing strategy.

Google Analytics can monitor a variety of conversions and pre-defined user goals and becomes the basis for defining and tracking conversions. It is a very effective strategy to allow for multiple online conversion points because web users prefer to convert through different means.

Conversion Examples

Any visit to a website which results in some form of interaction with the website visitor is a conversion. There are many ways to measure a conversion on a website. Here are a few examples:

- Direct website visits and targeted page visits
- Inquiries via e-mail, phone or web-based forms.
- Visits to the Contact Us page
- A direct sale via the website
- E-mail newsletter subscriptions
- Viewing or reprinting driving directions
- PDF download or application submission
- Webinar or event registrations
- RSS subscription to podcasts and blogs
- Sending content to a friend or coworker
- A phone call from a dedicated website phone number
- A form submission to receive something free
- An e-mail to the company from the website
- Driving out to your store or office
- Sending a link to a friend or referring a friend
- Viewing multimedia on the website

- Making an online donation or pledge
- Printing a coupon from the website

This is not a complete list and conversions are only limited by one's imagination, business needs and user intentions.

E-commerce Versus Lead Generation

The vast majority of conversions fall into the two broad categories of either direct online purchases or lead generation. Most readers of this book will be primarily looking to generate leads from their online marketing efforts. All websites should make it very easy and intuitive to make contact. Keep in mind the Internet has replaced the phone book and many people will go to your website just to find a phone number and office hours.

In lead generation, the website content becomes the strategy. How you present and organize your online content will determine how well your site converts. Target a conversion rate of 1 to 2 percent. Follow-up or stay-in-touch programs will be critical to actually closing the lead. Without it, your web leads will not produce a return. More on stay-in-touch programs in later chapters. Use web content to develop a sales funnel and drive inquiries.

For e-commerce websites, the products become the strategy. Merchandising, or how products are presented, is critical. Follow best practices as there is no need to start from scratch. Understand seasonality and other online shopping trends and target a conversion rate of 2 to 4 percent for e-commerce sales. If you can sell directly online, then you should.

Website Usability Generates Conversions

Many websites are difficult to use and are actually barriers to online conversions. The easier your site is to use, the higher the conversion rate. User testing is a highly valuable form of market research that provides data for accomplishing this goal. Ask people to visit your website. Ask them what they are looking to find and give them tasks you can observe.

The solution is to be brave and keep it simple! Focus on two or three conversion points and include them on all web pages and especially navigation menus. Avoid heavy graphics, write in the language of the user and conduct user testing to verify your assumptions. Remember this formula: easy-to-use websites convert at higher rates.

Get Qualified Traffic to Increase Conversions

This should be obvious, but it is not, as most websites have bounce rates over 50 percent. It is better to have less traffic than the wrong traffic. Great content and a solid traffic generation strategy will achieve this goal. Review your stats to make sure the right traffic is coming to the website and realize that low conversion rates may mean poor traffic. Make sure your company value, benefits and focus are clear in the content throughout the site, and that search engine strategies match conversion goals.

It is common for web marketers to want more traffic, when many times what they really need is a better conversion rate. Set a goal of 3 to 5 percent of your website traffic converting. If this traffic is coming to you because they already know your brand, then set a goal of 5 to 10 percent of that traffic converting. More on traffic generation in coming chapters. Traffic generation is step three of the Four-Step Process.

Call to Action

All websites must have very clear call-to-action conversion points located near key content areas and in the main navigation. Thumbnails are a great design approach for combining content areas with call to action buttons or conversion links. Include a Contact Us or Buy Now button on every page or in every thumbnail.

Calls to action can be in taglines, captions, content, navigation systems and more. Follow best practices and meet the comfort level of your target market. Bigger is not always better, so avoid large ads or graphics to drive conversions. The best call to action on the site is your navigation menu and written content. Online submission forms that are simple and easy to complete can also be included on key content pages.

Forms and Content Sign Ups

Should website visitors have to sign up before you send them information? It depends, but it is not usually a good idea, because users don't like it. Test variations and see what happens. Giving away loads of free content is usually the best conversion tactic.

Follow this rule of thumb with submission forms: Shorter forms have higher conversion rates. Longer forms qualify the user more accurately and have lower conversion rates. Determine which is best for your business strategy.

Measure Conversions

Set up an account with Google Analytics and track conversions by the type of visitor. Develop an ROI method to calculate your sales revenue from web-based conversions. Google is very good at measuring conversions and setting up conversion paths, especially if you are running paid advertisements. Train marketing staff to look for these conversions and ask people how they heard about you and what motivated them to make contact.

All conversion points must be measured and tracked, including your e-commerce sales data. The bottom line with conversions is ROI and all conversions can be measured against ROI in great detail. We have an ROI tool on our website that can help you run the numbers on your website to determine ROI.

Try it out: www.intuitivewebsites.com/roi-calculator/

Tips to Generate More Website Conversions

Here are a few ideas for generating more conversions from your website:

- Website visitors are impulsive. Keep the content scannable and the links simple.
- Set the right message and call to action in your content.
- Place calls to action near popular content and on every page.
- Allow for more depth of content for analytical people.
- Shopping cart must be first rate, easy to use and intuitive.
- Use color photos with captions.
- Avoid objects that look like ads or large graphics. Online advertising is a turn-off.
- Customize landing pages for unique web search terms.
- Content and knowledge, not flash and graphics, drive conversions.
- Product photos on all pages and detailed descriptions are very important.
- Money back guarantees build trust.
- Call your website the official website.
- Use unique web phone numbers on every page.
- Include your e-mail address and contact form.
- Test special offers and incentives, especially free shipping.
- Is the motive of the website to sell stuff or help people?

- Draw qualified traffic from search engines.
- Have a professional, high quality design.
- Use consistent branding and messaging on the site.
- Be very well-organized in navigation and usability. This builds credibility.
- Load the website with content and media that excites visitors.
- Have compelling offers that move people to action.
- Have a "Sign up now!" button for free content and newsletters.
- Be generous with your content. You will see results and more conversions.

SUMMARY

Conversions measure your success in winning the website war. The key is to track and measure web conversions and to make sure your website has one or more of these conversion strategies in place with call-to-action areas throughout each web page. Conversions are the beginning of a relationship and should place leads into a sales process that results in an ongoing relationship and develops a customer for your business. These are the web strategies that should be defined in your Internet marketing plan. They should be measured to set a conversion rate, an overall marketing ROI, and to exceed sales goals.

Test assumptions by asking for feedback from web visitors and with user testing.

Get creative and be realistic about results. When you have maximized your conversion rates, then work to get more traffic. Keep monitoring and improving your website to get better conversion results. Remember, your website is a constant salesperson for your company, and it is always under construction!

ACTION ITEMS

> Develop a web marketing plan that clearly identifies website conversions.

> Include in this plan a strategy and process for online conversions.

> Determine what conversions work best and set conversion rate goals.

> Develop an ideal path to conversions.

> Conduct user testing to verify assumptions.

> Schedule a weekly or monthly web conversion meeting with your team.

> Review your top performing competitors across industries.

> Test various ideas and offers.

> Use unique web-based phone numbers on your site for tracking.

> Watch your stats weekly or monthly on Google Analytics.

> Develop conversion points based on estimated ROI.

> Track website activity toward ROI goals.

TRUE STORY – Only the Names Have Been Changed to Protect Privacy

"I know the website is working for us because I can see the increase in phone calls, e-mails and new business signups. This was not happening before we launched the new website," says John Walker the CEO of American Lock Company.

"Before we started working on our web marketing strategy we did not give much thought to our website," says Walker. "We did not think our target market used the internet. We were wrong about that."

American Lock Company is a manufacturer of custom keyless entry systems for very specific target markets. Their website has become a major source of leads for the sales team and has been the key to business growth.

The company developed a professional website with clear instructions about the buying process. This resulted in a dramatic increase in submissions and requests for products. The site has a conversion rate of 2 percent and traffic has doubled in the past two years. Both new customers and the activation of lapsed customers is driving this trend. A mobile website was also developed as 25 percent of site visitors were coming from mobile devices.

"We did not think that so many of our inactive customers would use the website to place new orders and reactivate their accounts," continued John. "This has really helped us get current customers to reorder in larger numbers than we expected. It also keeps them away from our competitors. We saved a lot of money by getting rid of a 50,000-piece mailer and focusing on the website."

Here is what American Lock Company learned from the Four-Step Process:

Strategy: Build a professional website–without making assumptions about how people use it–that clearly explains the buying process to new prospects and to customers looking to reorder. Make strategic decisions based on web data.

Design and Development: Use the website to educate and teach current customers how to place orders. Include content in a variety of areas related to the industry and the needs of the target market.

Traffic Generation: Target SEO for the company brand and related terms used by actual customers to find the company. Develop linking strategies from key association websites used by the target market.

Monitoring ROI and Tracking Results: Meet monthly to review web stats and how conversions happen from the website. Continue to simplify content to improve conversions.

The Results: Steady growth in revenues from an increase in former customers placing new orders and reactivating their accounts.

CHAPTER

STEP THREE: Traffic Generation

Website traffic generation, step three of the Four-Step Process, is by far the most popular of the four steps and certainly gets the most attention. Every company wants as much traffic as possible to their website and to be on the first page of Google search results for their targeted terms. Many web marketing agencies make traffic generation and getting results in Google their key selling point.

We have found in the past fifteen years of web marketing it is the combination of the four steps, driven by an excellent strategy, that drives online results. Just getting traffic is not a complete solution, and can be expensive because traffic generation takes time and money. Traffic generation is important, but does not stand alone as the key ingredient to success with web marketing.

Traffic Generation Requires Hard Work

Drawing visitors to your website has become a fairly level playing field over time. New websites struggle to capture the amount of visitors that go to older, more well-established sites. It takes time to build traffic. The amount of time and money put into getting traffic is in many ways equal to the amount of work you put into it. There is no quick fix or special treatment given to any particular websites. The hard work put into building traffic should have excellent ROI. This book will help you develop a traffic generation strategy to drive business growth.

Search Engines and Traffic Generation

Traffic from Google searches and direct traffic are the two most likely sources of website visitors for most sites. Many people use Google instead of their browser to find a website, even if they know the company name or domain name of the site.

There is more to traffic generation than search engines. In fact, search engines such as Google require you to pay attention to many factors so you can be found in their search results. Although direct traffic is great, business growth will generally come from people experiencing your brand for the first time through a Google search.

A Comprehensive Approach to Traffic Generation

Just as web marketing in general needs a comprehensive approach, so does step three (traffic generation). As we move into the upcoming chapters on website visitor growth, keep in mind all these efforts work together to grow traffic from a variety of sources.

CHAPTER

The Fundamentals of Website Traffic Generaion

Business leaders must have an understanding of the fundamentals of website traffic generation and what drives traffic to their company website. The good news: traffic generation to your website can be easily summarized for a few key traffic sources. Remember, traffic generation is step three of the Four-Step Process. Drive traffic to your website after the strategy is in order and the design is great. Driving traffic costs money and time, so it is not a good idea to drive traffic to a website that is not optimized for success.

Website traffic sources can be broken down into three major areas.

THREE MAJOR TRAFFIC SOURCES

Google Analytics breaks down the sources of website traffic into three major areas: direct traffic, search engine traffic and referral traffic. Here is an overview of each one.

1. Direct Traffic

This is traffic that comes to your website by typing in your website URL or domain name into their browser or from a bookmarked page on the site visitor's web browser. Direct traffic is an indicator of your brand's popularity on the Internet and will usually have the highest conversion rates. Much of this traffic is generated by word of mouth and from offline marketing efforts.

It is always a good idea to have a domain name that matches your company name. For example, if your company name is ABC Widgets your website should be ABCWidgets.com. This will make it much easier for direct traffic to find you. Otherwise, you may end up sending direct traffic to a competitor's website.

2. Search Engine Traffic

This is traffic that comes to your website from a search in a major search engine. It can be from organic results in the free listings, social media or from paid advertisements. Much of your traffic will come from searches on your company name, which makes this traffic similar to direct traffic.

Search engines should drive at least 50 percent of your overall traffic and you should work hard to be listed on the first page of Google search results for the keyword terms most appropriate for your company. Google is the leading search engine by far and has a more than 70 percent search engine market share.

3. Referral Traffic

The third form of traffic is referral traffic. This is traffic that comes from another website through a link to your website. At one time, this was an important factor in search engine rankings, but it is now an indicator of your site's online reach and your ability to build a partnership with websites that attract your target market.

FIVE TRAFFIC GENERATION AREAS OF FOCUS

We can go one step further and break down your traffic generation efforts into five key areas of focus for the web marketing team. These areas will be discussed in more detail in coming chapters, and here is an overview.

1. Offline Sales and Marketing

For most companies, the most valuable traffic comes from those who know your brand, are current customers or have been referred to your website. This traffic will be listed as "direct traffic" in Google Analytics or they will use your company name to find your site in a search engine. Make it easy for people to find your website by including your domain name on all your company materials and on any items that are seen by your target market. Do not get so caught up in your web marketing work that you forget to give attention to offline marketing efforts that drive very qualified traffic to your site.

2. Search Engines

Search engine traffic is one of the best sources for new customers and can be broken into two areas. The first is organic traffic coming from your search engine optimization (SEO) efforts. This is the traffic displayed in the free search results. The second form of search engine traffic is from pay-per-click (PPC) ad programs, such as Google AdWords. Traffic from search engines consists of brand name searches and new targeted searches based on keyword research and SEO. Many people use Google to find your website by searching your company name. You will learn more about SEO in upcoming chapters.

3. Content Marketing

Content marketing is a key part of search engine results, but also a traffic generation strategy in its own right. Users will come to your site for valuable content and it can be used to pull targeted traffic from a variety of sources. The key is to have a content marketing plan to drive these results. E-mail marketing, your online content, blogs and other content types are examples of content marketing.

4. Social Media

Social media is one of the best interactive channels for content distribution and traffic generation. It is also important for SEO and branding. Social media websites such as Facebook and LinkedIn have become so large that they can be considered their own version of the Internet! There is also a lot of hype associated with social media and it is important to set the right expectations and goals for social media results. It is also one of the fastest changing parts of web marketing.

5. Partnerships and Links from Relevant Websites

It is important to see links coming to your site as partnerships with other websites and not as link exchanges or search engine bait. There should be a reason to have links to your website and you should reach out to appropriate websites to request a link. Google continues to rank websites with inbound links higher in search results, although this is not as critical to your SEO efforts as it was in the past.

SUMMARY

Take time to understand the five key areas of traffic generation. You do not need to be an expert in each area. Only a broad understanding is needed so you can ask the right questions and make sure traffic generation is in alignment with your overall web marketing strategy. The majority of your website traffic will come as a result of work in those five areas.

ACTION ITEMS

➤ Include a traffic generation plan for each of these five areas in your overall web marketing plan. Remember to include offline marketing in these efforts.

➤ Make sure each area is coordinated with the web marketing strategy.

➤ Check assumptions with your website data in each area through your Google Analytics reports and stats.

➤ Learn more about content marketing and develop a plan for content to drive website traffic.

➤ Understand the social networks frequented by your target market and develop a strategy to reach them with content posts.

➤ Learn how to research keywords and the fundamentals of SEO.

➤ Develop a list of websites that should link to your website and pursue a linking strategy with those companies.

CHAPTER 30

How Offline Marketing Contributes to Online Success

U nless you are strictly an online business, which most companies are not, the single biggest contributor to online marketing success is what you do offline. Your company's brand and reputation will drive the most qualified traffic to your website that will convert at the highest levels. Ultimately, your website supports your overall sales and marketing strategy and must be in alignment with what you do offline to maximize results. Yes, offline marketing helps you win at online marketing! Here are a few things to consider when aligning your online and offline marketing efforts.

Pay Attention to Web Marketing

The company website is easy to ignore because it is not usually a part of the routine of the business owner or leader. You can make it a part of your regular sales and marketing work by reviewing web stats on a regular basis and scheduling a web marketing meeting at least once a month. Use these meetings and web stats to ask questions about web strategy and how it impacts the company's overall marketing plan. Your web stats must be seen as a key business indicator to be reviewed on a regular basis.

Website Domain Name

Most people will look for your website domain name as the first step to visiting your website. They expect the domain name to match the company name and this should be an exact match. This is very important because you can actually send web traffic to your competitors by using a domain name that does not match your company name. We have consulted with many companies where this was the case, and they were sending traffic to a competitor's website because of a poorly chosen domain name.

For example, if your company name is Standard Manufacturing, but your domain name is **www.StandardInc.com**, you will be sending traffic to **www.StandardManufacturing.com**.

If a competitor has that domain name, then they will get your web traffic regardless of their actual company name. In fact, much of their web traffic will come from your offline marketing efforts and referrals!

This is so important in today's world of marketing that you should consider changing your company name to match an available domain name. Also, it is better to have a long domain name that is your full company name, rather than a shorter domain name that is cryptic and hard to remember. This makes it easier for people to refer others to your company.

Put Your Website Domain on Everything

Anything that is printed or visible to prospective customers should include your domain name. This includes invoices, packaging, vehicles, buildings and other parts of your business that are seen by prospective customers. This will drive qualified website traffic.

Coordinate Web Marketing with the Sales Team

Your sales team has a unique vantage point in understanding your website visitors. Web marketing efforts should be coordinated with the sales team. You will find some salespeople to be excellent web marketers. They do this by offering website design options, preparing online content, running social media programs and more. They should at least have input into web marketing efforts and regularly attend web marketing meetings. As prospecting becomes more difficult, more sales professionals will gravitate to online marketing as an important lead generation tactic. An entire chapter of this book has been devoted to this subject, as it is growing in importance for sales and marketing teams.

The Website as an Extension of the Sales Process

Your website must be seen as an extension of your sales process. The sales team is talking to prospects and customers every day. They are in the best position to understand what motivates website users to become sales leads and how to develop a conversion process that seamlessly transitions the lead into their sales process.

The Internet is the biggest source of leads for many companies, and prospecting, or push marketing, has transitioned to content marketing, or pull marketing, to drive inquiries and sales leads. Get the sales team involved in the process to drive results and improve ROI.

What Works Offline Works Online

Sales and marketing tactics that work offline should be translated to the web and monitored. This can include promotions, pricing strategies, advertising campaigns, media resources and more. Look at what has driven the success of your company over time offline and translate those tactics to your website. This is set in motion with excellent website content that users can easily find on the web.

SUMMARY

There is currently a blur between offline and online marketing. One of the biggest mistakes business leaders make is to ignore web marketing efforts because things are going well offline. Both work together to drive marketing results. It starts with making online marketing a part of your sales and marketing review and management process.

ACTION ITEMS

➤ Pay attention to your web marketing efforts and how they are coordinated with offline efforts. Have web stats sent to you once per week.

➤ Make sure your domain name exactly matches your company name.

➤ Put your website domain name on all your printed materials.

➤ Coordinate web marketing efforts with your sales team.

➤ See your website as an extension of your formal sales process.

➤ Find what works best offline and translate it to the Internet.

➤ Develop a web marketing plan and strategy for inbound marketing for lead generation.

CHAPTER 31

What is Inbound Marketing?

Inbound marketing is a key strategic focus at the core of many of the web marketing practices in this book. It is also known as pull marketing, and is at the heart of Internet marketing in general. Inbound marketing can be defined as the process of attracting targeted prospects to your company. Inbound marketing has always been around, and the Internet has become the major force behind its growth. For example, the Yellow Pages is a previous version of inbound marketing now replaced by Google searches.

Pull Versus Push

Many people confuse pull and push marketing. Push marketing is the idea of going out and finding customers through prospecting, cold calling, traditional selling and other techniques that begin with your sales and marketing team "pushing" prospects to you. Pull marketing is a strategy that involves creating an environment where customers find you and are "pulled," or attracted, to your company. Pull marketing is now a preference for most people as they research in anonymity online, and are very knowledgeable before they purchase or talk to a salesperson. The Internet is the biggest facilitator of pull marketing with its easy access to an abundance of information.

Most companies naturally gravitate to push marketing strategies. They are more comfortable with this approach because it is what they know best and it is what they have done in the past. Many marketers are looking for quick results from push marketing. Pull marketing can complement push marketing efforts and generate higher qualified leads, loyal followers and sales. The best advantage to pull marketing is the fact that most people prefer it to push marketing techniques as it better meets the needs of the online researcher. Pull marketing requires strategic planning, excellent content and solid tracking mechanisms.

Benefits of Pull Marketing

Here are a few of the benefits of effective pull marketing strategies:

- Can be used to target visitors to your website and social media

- Can be used to build a loyal following and excellent e-mail lists

- Leads to higher online conversion rates

- Opens up a wider net for people that would not have found your site otherwise

- Less costly than many forms of marketing, with a better ROI

Several key strategies must work together in order to gain these benefits. The first step is to make sure inbound marketing is a part of your web marketing plan. Also, the right team members must be recruited for inbound marketing along with a process for tracking results.

The Challenges of Inbound Marketing

Inbound marketing is not without its challenges. There is no quick fix, and inbound marketing can be time consuming. A higher level of marketing expertise will be needed, which may be lacking in your company. There will also be a learning curve to replace old habits. Inbound marketing requires written content, which can be time consuming and also requires a unique skill set. Overcoming these challenges has many positive results and is worth the time. Also, much of the work done to generate inbound marketing is permanently present on the web, and markets your business long after it first goes out to your target market.

The Company Culture and Inbound Marketing

Inbound marketing is the result of fundamental changes in sales and marketing brought on by the Internet. The sales and marketing culture of your company must embrace these approaches before they can take hold in your marketing efforts. They are not effective on a part-time basis or with limited buy-in from your team. Building the culture starts with inbound marketing education and is followed by implementation, tracking results and monitoring ROI.

Market Segmentation and Inbound Marketing

When well executed, strategic inbound marketing results in very specific market segmentation. This leads to better quality visits to your website, more leads, higher sales and more loyal followers. Forget mass market

approaches, and segment by online searches and search engi
research. Inbound marketing makes a small piece of pie very
because customers are more loyal and they come to you.

Use online research methods to identify your market segments and
develop "personas" for each of those segments. Personas are brief
descriptions of the people in that target market segment and how you
can best pull them to your company.

People want to be loyal to a brand because it makes life less
complicated. They don't have to repeatedly search through hundreds
of products and services to get what they need. The better you can
segment your target market and reach these personas, the better you
can create loyal customers for your brand and company. Inbound
marketing is the approach that pulls them to you.

The Death of Cold Calling in Sales

Cold calling may not be dead yet, but its effectiveness has dropped
substantially because people are now inundated with information,
and they want to buy on their terms. One way to deal with the
decline of cold calling is to convert salespeople to web marketers.
Find salespeople that have an inclination to web marketing and pull
marketing efforts, and put them to work on these new sales techniques.
Their time spent on pull marketing to generate sales leads will have a
strong return, if done properly.

Stay-in-Touch Programs

Inbound marketing will generate inquiries and leads, but it is your stay-
in-touch programs that work toward long-term sales results. Stay-in-
touch programs are reviewed in more detail in upcoming chapters and
must be included in an inbound marketing strategy.

SUMMARY

Take the time to learn more about how inbound marketing can
benefit your company. Begin with a cultural change in your
sales and marketing team so there is an emphasis on pulling
prospective customers to your company's website. We will go more
into this essential part of sales and marketing in the next chapter.

ACTION ITEMS

➤ Learn more about inbound marketing and include it in your web marketing plan.

➤ Assign team members to run an inbound marketing program and look to the sales team to build and support this work as needed.

➤ Answer these questions: Who are we trying to reach through inbound marketing? Where do they go online? How will they find us? What will motivate them to contact us?

➤ Include a strong and consistent content marketing strategy in your inbound marketing plan.

➤ Gather market research on what works with your current loyal customer base.

➤ Segment your market place into online buyer personas.

➤ Establish tracking systems and ROI measurement tools to track return.

➤ Make inbound marketing a part of your sales and marketing team culture.

➤ Include a stay-in-touch program as part of your inbound marketing strategy.

➤ Research your competitors' inbound marketing strategies along with those from other industries that can be applied to your company.

CHAPTER 32

Push Versus Pull Marketing and Website Traffic Growth

L et's dive deeper into the differences between pull and push marketing and how they impact traffic generation to your website and your overall web marketing efforts.

Pull and Push Marketing Defined

As we learned in the previous chapter, push marketing involves tactics such as finding customers through prospecting, cold calling, traditional selling and other techniques. It is the process of the sales and marketing team pushing prospects to the company. Pull marketing is a strategy that involves creating an environment where customers find you and are pulled, or attracted, to your company. Pull marketing is now a preference for most people as they research in anonymity online and are very knowledgeable before they purchase or talk to a sales person. These preferences have changed the traditional sales funnel and how companies should understand the new prospective customer.

People Prefer Pull Marketing Approaches

Prospective customers prefer pull marketing techniques. They want to research and find you, rather than getting a cold call, and the data supports pull marketing. Take a look at these findings from ThinkWithGoogle, a Google research study.

- 80 percent of consumers research before buying in business-to-consumer (B2C) markets.

- 57 percent of business-to-business (B2B) buyers research before making contact.

- Four out of five consumers use multiple devices to research, and mobile devices are a constant companion in their research.

139

- These numbers are increasing over time and are conservative estimates.

Your goal is to get found during their research on multiple devices, platforms and websites. This is the essence of pull marketing and the biggest differentiator from push marketing. Also, pull marketing requires that you know prospective customers very well.

Understanding the New Prospect

The Internet has influenced buying habits in many ways, and out of this has come a new, educated consumer and prospective buyer with many options. Here are a few key points to remember about the new consumer and your prospective customer in B2C and B2B markets.

- They scan content for value and will read on portable screens.

- They want quick, concrete, relevant and timely advice.

- Most just read; some want to comment or ask a question.

- They look for organized websites that they can trust.

- People are more important than companies or brands.

- They are very skeptical of what they don't know.

- They can see through the sizzle and marketing hype.

- They look for transparency to build trust.

The New Sales Funnel

The new sales prospect and the growth in pull marketing have resulted in a new sales funnel. The sales funnel is a visual representation of the actual steps in your company's sales process and selling cycle. It is large at the top because more time is spent on those action items and more people enter the funnel at the top than come out the bottom as buyers. The change toward an emphasis on pull marketing has led to a new sales funnel, as seen below.

The New Sales Funnel

In this new sales funnel, prospecting is replaced by lead generation from pull marketing strategies that generate qualified leads, much of this coming from online marketing. These leads are educated about your services and products by reading your content and contacting you once they establish value. Your content should be plentiful, relevant and available on the web.

Qualifying your target market is much more focused and based on self-service research efforts from your target market. This is driven by content marketing. Your presentations are very targeted and customized to the prospect's needs. Any prospects that fall out of the funnel at any time should become part of your stay-in-touch program. Closing takes less effort, is a natural part of the process and is not forced. This is a new approach to selling milestones and the sales process is brought on by pull marketing. Share this information with your sales team and use it to coordinate efforts between sales and marketing.

Salespeople as Content Experts

Salespeople should become web marketing content experts. Whether they are writing blog posts, networking in social media or performing a variety of content marketing tasks, their customer and company knowledge is essential to pull marketing success. Not all salespeople will succeed at this and many will have nothing to do with writing content or marketing online. However, you may find hidden gems in your sales team that love online marketing and can make your pull marketing very successful. Finding a strong salesperson who loves to write is key to this strategy.

SUMMARY

By not paying attention to pull marketing, it is possible that your company will see declining sales and lost market share without being aware of why it is happening. Your targeted buyers will migrate to competitors that have implemented effective pull marketing strategies. Stay ahead of your competition and make pull marketing an engine of sales and marketing growth for your company. Also, don't stop selling or using push marketing tactics that work. Keep in mind that it is the coordination of efforts between push and pull marketing that can lead to excellent results and help you win the website war.

ACTION ITEMS

> Educate your sales and marketing teams about pull and push marketing strategies.

> Develop your sales funnel with key milestones based on pull marketing approaches and strategies.

> Set targets and goals for each step in the process.

> Include this in your content marketing and web marketing plans.

> Share this information with your sales team and recruit their help with implementation.

> Visit competitor websites and evaluate how they are using pull marketing techniques.

> Research your "new" prospective customers to understand how they will research your company online and what will motivate them to contact your company.

CHAPTER 33

Everything the Business Leader Needs to Know About Search Engines

When most people think of web marketing, the first thing that comes to mind is getting found in search engines, most likely Google. Here are the key points business leaders need to know about search engines as part of their comprehensive web marketing plan and strategies.

No Quick Fix

The first and most important thing to know about search engine marketing is that there is no quick fix! It takes time, effort and strategy to get results in the search engines. Putting in the time and effort almost always generates results, but you may never be number one for the terms you desire. That does not mean you can't be successful and get a large amount of targeted traffic over time. Search engine optimization (SEO) is a long-term marketing effort that requires patience and careful tracking to produce results.

Google Dominates

Google has almost all the market share among the most popular search engines. This could change, but as of 2014 and the near future, Google has well over 70 percent market share among the major search engines. MSN and Yahoo make up most of the remaining market share. The vast majority of your qualified search engine web traffic will come from Google. The primary search engine focus of this book is on getting found in Google. The good news is that what works in Google tends to work in other search engines as well.

Google as a Branding Tool

Getting found in Google is more than just getting traffic to your website. It is also about your company's brand. Research and target the right keywords and then make sure you are on the first page of Google for those search terms. The branding impact is as important as the actual website traffic and you may have to use Google AdWords to get listed in these searches.

Google AdWords

AdWords is Google's online advertising service displaying paid ads in search results. It is the reason Google is highly profitable, and one of the most valued companies in the world. For these reasons alone, business leaders should learn more about AdWords. You can read more about Google AdWords and pay-per-click (PPC) advertising in upcoming chapters.

Prospecting and Google

Google search results have replaced prospecting and cold calling. People want to find you in search results during their online research. This has replaced cold calling and other push marketing techniques. Remember, it is more effective to pull qualified prospects into your website than to go knocking on doors, hoping prospects will make time to talk with you. They will make contact with your company when they find your website by targeted web searches.

Keyword Research

Use the Google keyword planning tool found in AdWords to determine the keywords most appropriate for your website. Select the keywords used by your target market. Keep in mind these keywords may not be your first choice because most people research the terms they think best fit their needs. These may not be the terms you thought they would be. Also, if you find there are too many keywords and it is overwhelming, organize your keywords by market segments or keyword themes. Google's keyword tool can help with this process.

THE FOUR KEY AREAS OF SEARCH ENGINE OPTIMIZATION (SEO)

There are four important areas to address when optimizing your website for Google searches. Your keywords should be implemented in these four areas:

1. Website Code

Keywords should be strategically placed in the code of your website. This code is not visible on your website pages. The code can be seen in web searches, at the top of your browser, when you mouse over a photo and in other ways, but not in the actual web page content. The code includes title tags, meta descriptions, headers, alt tags and related code.

2. Website Content

The appropriate keywords must also be in your website content and must complement the keyword strategy used in your website code. This is the content read by your website visitors. Regular content updates are important along with a blog that includes optimized code and content.

3. Links from Other Websites

Google made its mark as a search engine by using website link popularity as a key part of its ranking process. Websites with more links from important websites ranked higher in search results. This popularity approach made results more relevant and is still important today, although Google has placed less emphasis on this recently, in favor of content. At a minimum, have several high-traffic websites linking to your website. It is best to make this an organic process and ask for the links.

4. Authorship and Content Leadership

Google respects content leadership, and improved search engine results go hand-in-hand with the credibility of the content's author. This is why a Google+ account is important and necessary to improve search results. Make sure your content is appearing in Google+ and work to position yourself as a content leader in your marketplace. More on Google+ in upcoming chapters on social media.

Google Webmaster Tools

This Google tool is essential to SEO results and the only method available to communicate directly with Google and track Google bots (also known as spiders) as they index your website in the Google search database. This is the software run by Google to rank your website in Google search results. Google also uses Webmaster Tools to help prevent spam and track malware. One of Google's major priorities is to prevent spam websites from showing up in search results. Sites that have a Webmaster Tools account are less likely to be spammer websites.

SUMMARY

Hopefully this book is teaching you that there is much more to web marketing than getting found in Google. Yet, it is very important to have a basic understanding of how Google works and the steps needed to get results in online web searches. You can use this knowledge to help direct your search engine optimization (SEO) staff and better understand what they are doing to drive traffic from the search engines.

ACTION ITEMS

➤ Make time to learn the basics of search engine optimization (SEO) and Google.

➤ Compile a list of search engine keywords that you want to be listed on the first page of Google, and drive your web marketing team to make that happen. Some keywords may be too competitive, so look for niches and conduct local searches as needed.

➤ Make sure all four steps of SEO are covered on your current website.

➤ Research and learn more about Google AdWords and run a few test campaigns to get hands-on training with AdWords.

➤ Set up and review Google Webmaster Tools.

➤ Select someone to be your website and blog content authority. This may be you!

CHAPTER 34

Understanding Google AdWords and Other Pay-Per-Click Services

In the early days of the Internet, a search engine called GoTo.com began running ads alongside their organic or natural search results. These ads were sold through an automated auction and bidding system, and advertisers were only charged if they received clicks on their ads, which linked to the advertiser's website. The top placement in search results went to the highest bidder. Bidding started at a penny per click. This became known as pay-per-click (PPC) advertising because the advertiser's account was charged only when someone clicked on the ad and visited the advertiser's website.

GoTo.com changed its name to Overture.com, and was eventually bought by Yahoo. Their software still powers the Yahoo paid search program now run by the Bing search engine from MSN (MicroSoft).

While the concept of PPC ads and auction bidding was started by GoTo.com and expanded by Yahoo, it was actually Google that took this to an entirely new level of popularity and success with Google AdWords. Millions of advertisers began using AdWords and Google revenues exploded. AdWords is what makes Google profitable and one of the most valuable companies on the planet. Google leveraged the popularity of their search engine to sell new AdWords accounts and drive incredible sales growth. AdWords allowed any website to attract large amounts of visitors, as long as they could afford the click charges from Google ads.

Google AdWords continues to be a viable online marketing resource with excellent ROI when pursuing specific target markets and keyword niches. The most successful Google AdWords campaigns are highly targeted and carefully matched to the keyword searches most likely to result in sales.

How to Get Started with AdWords

The first step is to set up an AdWords account with Google. It is free and you can use the same login for AdWords as any other Google app, such as Google Analytics, Gmail and others. In fact, it works best when all your Google apps are set up under one account. This starts by securing a Gmail e-mail account for your company and this e-mail address can be used for all your Google account logins.

Following the AdWords account signup, you will need to set up your campaigns and segments for each campaign called AdGroups. These segments are very important because of how you will select keywords and prepare ads. It also forces you to segment your online marketplace, which brings value to all your marketing efforts. The final steps are to write ads and select keywords.

Here are a few recommendations from our many years of AdWords experience:

- Keep your ads very simple and very direct.

- Set up unique website landing pages for your ads.

- Include a call to action in your ads.

- Test three or four ads per AdGroup.

- It is better to have more AdGroups than ads.

- Use keyword research to segment and establish AdGroups.

- Include negative keywords to avoid unwanted clicks.

- Some keywords can dominate results and must be segmented.

- Your ads will display based on your bids and Google's relevancy.

- Link AdWords to your Google Analytics account and track conversions.

There are many tools and reports associated with AdWords and a very good help section with videos. Take time to review this information and watch the AdWords videos on the Google AdWords website.

Target to Get Results

There are three principle methods for targeting qualified traffic in AdWords: keyword selections, ads and user location. When done correctly, this is where the genius of AdWords can produce results for just about any website. Use keywords and ads to specifically target exactly what will bring results for your website. Also, AdWords gets results by complementing organic search and gives your website an opportunity to be seen in multiple places on the first page of Google search results. Targeting by location provides an opportunity to target any location in the world and better control your budget. In many cases, this is a key to excellent ROI from AdWords.

Use AdWords for Market Research

The data that comes from a live AdWords campaign is incredibly insightful. Even if you don't produce many leads or sales, the data alone is worth the investment. You will see an exact number of searches for each keyword and the popularity of your ads in those search results. Ads should convert at 1 to 2 percent of impressions from searches, and high performing ads can have a click-through rate as high as 10 percent. This data is very useful and will provide feedback to many other parts of your sales and marketing programs. In fact, Google may start providing less information for free through Google Analytics and relying on marketers to set up AdWords accounts to get search data. As of this writing in early 2014, it is already happening with keyword search data in Google Analytics.

Google throws out a very broad net, so make sure to target your keyword setting and include negative keywords to avoid paying for the wrong type of traffic.

What is the Cost of AdWords?

The total budget spent in AdWords is based on your expected return. Whether it is the benefits of market research or direct sales, AdWords should result in solid ROI. Your ROI results are driven by how well you implement your AdWords strategy. Your budget may be as low as $50 per month to get value for AdWords.

Perform a Google search in your industry and see if competitors are using AdWords. More than likely, their ads can be found running in AdWords because they are getting results with an acceptable ROI. They get those results because the advertiser has total control over their AdWords budget. This is true whether you spend thousands of dollars or just a few hundred. This almost-guaranteed ROI from a well-run AdWords program is the best reason to test AdWords as a part of your web marketing plan.

SUMMARY

Do your research and learn more about AdWords. Many companies fail at AdWords because they go too broad and expect too much. Keep your campaigns very targeted and closely track results. Make a commitment to include AdWords in your web marketing plan and make an effort to set up campaigns with a solid ROI. Follow the guidelines in this chapter and make use of AdWords as an excellent weapon to win the website war.

ACTION ITEMS

➤ Set aside a test budget and establish a targeted AdWords campaign.

➤ Search in Google to find your competitors in AdWords and determine their strategy. They may have a few good ideas you can copy.

➤ Focus on targeted keywords and simple direct ads with a solid call to action.

➤ Link your AdWords to Google Analytics and track your results.

➤ Don't worry, competitors can't drain your AdWords budget by repeatedly clicking on your ads. Google has set up tracking methods to prevent this.

➤ Contact Google directly for help with AdWords at 877-906-7955.

CHAPTER 35

The Importance of E-mail Marketing

Most small businesses don't use e-mail to market their products and services. They are missing out on what may be the most cost-effective form of online marketing available. It is common for business leaders to see e-mail marketing as spam, but the reality is loyal customers and targeted prospects are looking for valuable content that can improve the quality of their lives or make their job easier. E-mail allows you to meet those needs and reach thousands of targeted subscribers in a way that is unmatched by other forms of direct marketing. Here are the steps to get started with e-mail marketing.

Build a Great List

The very best e-mail lists include people who voluntarily sign up (opt-in) for your e-mail marketing program. Another good source are e-mail addresses collected from online sources such as your website and social media. E-mail marketing success will always be based on the strength of your e-mail list and the value subscribers get from your e-mail content. Purchased e-mail lists do not usually bring enough value in building a great list of loyal followers. In addition, using a purchased list is likely to upset people who feel they are being spammed. We don't recommend using your e-mail list to prospect for new business by including people that have no connection to your company.

Make it easy for website visitors to sign up for your e-mail blasts on your website. Your list should comprise loyal followers, current customers, referral sources, prospective customers and others who know your company. Start with those that know your company best and build a great e-mail list. Some people will obviously ask to be removed from your list or unsubscribe. Don't dwell on these people, as they will usually be a small percentage of the overall list.

E-mail Signup Box

Place an easy-to-find e-mail signup box on your website, if possible on the upper left corner of the site. This allows for easy access from your most loyal followers and those most likely to subscribe. E-mail subscribes can be tracked in Google Analytics and this should be seen as a key conversion point for your website.

Prepare Excellent E-mail Content

E-mails with poor content are deleted or go to spam. E-mails with excellent content will be read, distributed around the web and will drive website visits and online conversions. Write desirable content in e-mails. This includes content that helps people do their jobs better or improves the quality of their lives. It should also include a strong call to action and/or promotions. The graphic design of your e-mail blast should be appropriate for your target market. Many e-mail marketers make the mistake of over-designing their e-mail blasts, and this leads to low response rates as most people prefer content over graphics. Interesting photos and valuable content will draw e-mail subscribers to your company.

Monthly E-mail Marketing

The frequency of your marketing e-mails depends upon your online strategy; however, once per month is a good target for most e-mail blasts and newsletters. This is enough frequency to stay top-of-mind with subscribers, but not too much, which is annoying.

Coordinate E-mail Marketing with Social Media, Blogs and other Content

E-mail newsletter campaigns work best when coordinated with social media and blogs. Content and special promotions sent in your marketing e-mails should also be included in social media. Also, make sure to archive all your e-mail newsletters on your website and code them for SEO purposes. Allow website visitors to subscribe to your blog posts and your e-mail newsletters and announcements.

Track and Measure E-mail Results

There are dozens of very good e-mail marketing providers with excellent tracking capabilities. Programs like MailChimp, ConstantContact, iContact and others are easy to use and have excellent reporting tools that often link to Google Analytics. These tools will cover the bases needed to make sure your e-mail campaigns follow the rules and drive success. These software tools have excellent pricing, and are easy to set up to deal with subscribing and unsubscribing issues.

SUMMARY

If done correctly, there are very few downsides and many upsides to running a monthly e-mail marketing program. A few people may unsubscribe, but the vast majority of people will appreciate your valuable e-mail content, especially if they are loyal followers or customers. This connection with your e-mail content will drive sales. Take the time to make e-mail marketing a part of your web marketing strategy and your content marketing plan.

ACTION ITEMS

➤ Set up an account with an e-mail marketing service such as MailChimp.

➤ Add an e-mail signup box to your website.

➤ Make a list of e-mail topics that help your target market do their job better or improve the quality of their lives.

➤ Make a list of e-mail promotions and calls to action that have worked in the past (offline or online).

➤ Assign a content writer to prepare brief, informative e-mails.

➤ Make use of excellent photography with captions in e-mail blasts.

➤ Make sure subscribers can easily opt-out of your e-mail lists.

➤ Plan a monthly marketing e-mail and track results in your web stats.

CHAPTER 36

How Content Marketing Drives Website Traffic and Conversions

One of the most powerful forms of online marketing is called "content marketing." Content marketing is the strategy and process behind using your online content to draw people to your company and converting them into customers. It is very strategic and has become an essential part of any company's marketing efforts. Content marketing is driven by people's need for information before they make a purchasing decision and is behind the growth in pull marketing.

THE CONTENT MARKETING PROCESS: TEN STEPS

More than likely, your marketing department is already doing some form of content marketing. Most companies wing it and do the best they can with content marketing. However, the lack of a strategic process impedes their results. Content marketing will get much better results with a strategic process that has proven to be successful. Here are ten steps in that process.

1. Write for the Reader

The most common mistake of content marketers is to write from the perspective of their own company instead of using language that is easily understood by their target market. Each organization has an internal language, a set of terms and methods for communicating that works for their company, but this may not be how prospective customers communicate. The first step in content marketing is to bridge the gap between the company and the reader.

Write content to help your target market do their job better and improve the quality of their lives. Use quality thinking and avoid marketing speak or brochure content. Write content with value and that educates, and avoid content that sells or self-promotes.

2. Use Content Marketing to Get Found in Google

The more content on your website, the better your rank in Google searches. Google is paying more attention to websites with blogs and regular content updates. Here are a few points directly from Google to consider in regard to content marketing and search results.

- 500 to 1,000 web pages is ideal for most websites.
- Adding fifty pages to your site is equal to 48 percent more search engine traffic.
- Your website gets nine times more traffic when you reach 1,000 pages.
- Websites with blogs get five times more traffic than those without blogs.
- The more content on your site, the better rank it will have in Google searches.

Also, being on the first page of a Google search result is important branding for your business. A key element in sales prospecting today has become Google searches or people researching the online marketplace to find your company. Keyword searches and content optimized for Google will bring loyal customers to your website. Your content marketing strategy drives this process.

3. Content as the Voice of the Brand

Many writers may contribute to your web content marketing efforts, but it is important to have one consistent voice for your company brand. This builds trust and drives simplicity for readers as they learn more about your products and services. Content marketing is used to explain your value to your target markets, and consistency is critical to communicate a clear brand message. This content provides a personality to your brand and the consistency leads to better marketing results.

4. Translate What You Do Well into Online Content

Get very specific on product and service content that is unique to your company. Write about what your company does well. Website visitors will appreciate this because it is what they are looking for. What you do well is loaded with benefits, and content should be used to explain this, including videos, photos, graphics, audio and other media. Tell the story of what you do and how you do it. Also, remember that marketing verbiage and ads are not usually perceived as valuable content.

5. Make Content a Competitive Advantage

There is a new definition of free content and it is your "competitive advantage." In other words, giving content away for free has become a competitive advantage. Many companies resist this because they believe they are giving away their secrets. However those secrets are not as important as you think. If you don't give them away, others will. The upside beats the downside; you are only hiding value if you don't distribute excellent content. Your web marketing and lead generation strategy determines how much to give away. Anyone can compete with content and if you don't, others will, which will take away online market share, and you may not even see it happening!

6. Write Great Headers and Taglines

Headers, taglines and photo captions are the most read content on the Internet. This content should be direct, simple and catchy for visitors that will scan your website looking for areas of value to them. When website visitors see the benefit in headers and taglines, they will pursue deeper content for more information. Excellent headers and taglines save people time and create value.

7. Communicate in Layers

Website visitors scan content quickly. You can meet their needs by using taglines, headers, and short blocks of text on key landing pages as scannable content. The website reader should be able to go deeper into your site and find volumes of content and information as needed, but they will only find this content if they can first scan and search.

Set up your content in layers on your website. Taglines and brief bullet points with links to more information are best to accomplish this goal, in addition to an intuitive navigation menu. Keep your content brief on the key landing pages of your website. Most website content can be cut in half and still communicate the same message.

Websites provide an opportunity for almost limitless amounts of content to meet visitor needs. Origin this content in layers so users can first scan and then dig deeper to find volumes of content. An added benefit is improved search results from Google and other search engines.

8. Always Use Captions with Photos and Graphics

Photos are by far the most-looked-at content on the Internet. Photos without captions tell different stories to each person that sees that photo. Always write clear and direct captions for all your website photography so that ten out of ten people can easily understand the photo's message and the purpose of the photo on your website. Avoid clip art and stock photography, as this can be seen as clutter. You can often find the same stock photo on many different websites and this creates brand confusion. Use real photos of real people and things at your company, along with a caption on each photo. This will likely be the most valuable content on your website and get the most attention from visitors.

9. Watch the ROI on Content Marketing

Overall, content marketing is cheaper than traditional advertising and many other forms of marketing. Still, you should set up tracking methods to monitor conversions and track the ROI from content marketing, and all web marketing efforts, for that matter. Content marketing should have excellent and measurable ROI. Content marketing is also more permanent than most forms of sales and marketing because content placed online will be there for a long time.

10. Create a Company Culture for Content Marketing

This is especially important in order for sales and marketing staff and top leadership to embrace content marketing. Writing and preparing content is hard work, and support must come from top levels of the organization. The transition to content marketing from traditional push marketing can be difficult and will take leadership. Start by using the content around the office that can be rewritten for the web. Improved marketing results will help drive the culture needed to implement a winning content marketing strategy.

Barriers to Content Marketing

There are many barriers to content marketing and most people avoid it as much as possible. Many people in sales and marketing have not developed the necessary writing skills to be effective in content marketing. Here are a few of the common barriers you will need to overcome.

- Don't have the time or the people
- The team will have to work too hard
- Giving away free content will not work for the company
- The wrong skill set in the marketing or sales staff
- Many people hate to write
- Unable to relate to the customer or understand online prospecting

Don' let these barriers to content marketing get in the way of your online success. Find the right people and build a team to implement content marketing strategies.

SUMMARY

Content marketing covers a lot of ground, and is a new form of prospecting for sales. It is at the core of pull marketing and a driver of inbound marketing strategies. You can read more about blogs, types of content and content marketing channels in later chapters. In many ways, content marketing is the most important tactic in driving traffic to your website, and Google is leading the charge in responding to effective content marketing strategies.

ACTION ITEMS

➤ Include a content marketing strategy in your web marketing plan.

➤ Meet with your key sales and marketing staff and develop a process for content marketing as a regular part of your web marketing efforts.

➤ Assign the content marketing work to people who show initiative and want to write. Some of these people may be outside contractors.

➤ Understand and segment the audience for each form of content.

➤ Determine your content outlets, types and topics.

➤ Assign a team member to schedule content placement in various channels.

➤ Make sure all content is optimized for the search engines.

➤ Develop a schedule for regular content placement and updates.

➤ Track results and conversion rates to determine your ROI.

CHAPTER 37

How Business Blogs and Content Drive Traffic

Blogs are at the core of a successful content marketing program and just about every website should have a blog. Here are a few key points business leaders need to know about developing a blog marketing strategy.

Blogs Drive Website Traffic

Google loves websites with blogs and regular content posts. Websites with blogs get five times more traffic than similar sites without blogs. This is reason enough to have a blog. However, it becomes more compelling given the fact that website visitors like to read blog content as part of their research. Also, one of Google's major missions is to prevent spam websites from getting listed in their search results. Websites with regular blog posts and excellent content are not generally considered spam sites by Google.

Tell Your Company Story

Think of your company blog as an online content channel that tells the story of your company and unique marketplace on a regular schedule. It becomes an ongoing discussion about what it means to do business with your company and your marketplace in general. This is very helpful in defining and building your brand to the world. Here are a few key blog approaches used to get content marketing results.

- Place your blog on your main URL and do not use a separate website address or domain for the blog.

- Set a goal to write a new blog post every week, or daily, if possible.

- Keep blog posts brief and use headers to break up the text and for SEO purposes. All blog posts should be optimized for the search engines.

- Track visits to the blog in Google Analytics and monitor how your blog not only drives traffic, but also leads to conversions.

- Target about 400-600 words for each blog posting as a rule of thumb. It is fine to have some posts that are short and others that are much longer. The key is consistency and relevancy for your readers and for Google.

- Include share buttons to social media so readers can easily share your blog content with others.

If possible, include a link on your main navigation to your blog. This link may include other content resources such as articles, white papers, videos and more.

Begin with Blog Categories

Start your company blog by developing blog categories or a blog table of contents. This goes a long way in defining the purpose of your blog and how it will meet the needs of your readers. Here are a few ideas to help with developing blog categories.

- Tell the stories that happen at your business.

- Discuss industry issues in your blog.

- Write about your competitive advantages.

- Write about influential people or companies as they relate to your company.

- Discuss common problems and how to solve them for your target market.

- Include comparisons of products and services that matter to your target market.

- Review price issues in your blog.

- Conduct reviews of products and services.

- Write about the best of the past year.

- Include awards and company or industry news in your blog.

- Review competitor blog categories for ideas.

- Keep an archive for previous blog postings on your website.

Blog categories should include an archived category and the ability for the reader to search blog posts and organize the posts by date. Include at least four blog categories, and it is fine to have a generic category for miscellaneous postings.

Distribute Blog Content

Blogs and social media content should be interchangeable. All blog posts should be posted in social media and distributed through RSS feeds to blog subscribers. RSS is a technology that easily allows people to subscribe to your blog posts from your website and automatically receive blog content as it is posted on the site. This is an excellent way to distribute content that can be shared among your target market. The quality and value of this content will determine how it is shared and distributed around the Internet.

The About Us Page and Blog Content

Even though blog postings describe your company and marketplace in great detail, there is still need for an About Us page and it should be part of your main navigation. This could be one of the most important pages on your website, and will probably be in the top ten most visited pages on the site. Take the About Us page seriously, because this page can drive conversions. Here are a few key issues to address in your About Us pages:

- Use the About Us page to build trust and credibility.
- Think of it as the company resume.
- Include a link to this page in the main navigation menu.
- Keep the page current.
- Measure the stats and visits to this page.
- Include a conversion point and call to action on the About Us page.

Here are a few suggestions for the types of content to include on your About Us page:

- Company history
- Biographies and photos of team members
- Client lists, case studies and testimonials
- Location photos
- Videos and photos to describe your company
- Business approaches and philosophy of the company
- Other descriptive content about the company

Get Back What You Put In

Blogs take time and energy to be effective and the potential return is equal to the effort put into writing blog content. Just like many forms of web marketing discussed in this book, there is no quick fix; however, blog posts will get indexed within Google search results and will be read by your target market for years to come. This is true of any content posted to your website and a major benefit to a value-added content marketing strategy for your website.

SUMMARY

At the heart of your content marketing strategy will be your company blog. The blog is the one place for regular content on a variety of subjects. An active and interesting company blog takes advantage of your website's ability to be much more than a static, online brochure. Your site visitors and Google will appreciate your efforts. An excellent blog goes a long way toward winning the website war.

ACTION ITEMS

➤ Add a blog to your website under your main company URL.

➤ Determine a set of blog categories and subjects.

➤ Assign writing duties for a weekly or daily blog post.

➤ Use a consistent voice for the blog so there is no brand confusion.

➤ Keep blogs brief, code them for SEO and include a call to action.

➤ Link all blog postings in your social media content.

➤ Track the results as part of a comprehensive web marketing program.

Social Media Strategies for the Business Leader

Many millions of words and hundreds of books have been published on social media. Not a day goes by that a major media outlet is not discussing social media issues and events. The purpose of this chapter is to help business owners and leaders understand the strategy behind the use of social media as a web marketing channel. This chapter is not about the basics of social media or how business leaders should post on Facebook, or on other social media sites. Understanding social media strategy is important so that business leaders can provide the right direction to their sales and marketing teams.

No Quick Fix with Social Media

You will be disappointed in social media if you are looking for a quick fix or fast return. It takes time to build interest and followers. Without a loyal following, social media efforts can get very few results. Social media cannot stand on its own as an effective marketing channel. It is part of a comprehensive web marketing plan, content strategy and traffic generation program. Social media can be a very effective content channel to communicate your business strategy.

Welcome to the "Internets"

George W. Bush's famous line during his debate with John Kerry about the "Internets" has some truth to it. Social media websites like Facebook and LinkedIn have so many users these sites can easily be considered Internets within the Internet!

Your company's presence on a social media website starts with your company page, which is really another website for your company within the social media website. These social media company pages, or sites, should follow the same strategy as your company website. The design and content should complement your current website.

Social Media and Content Marketing

For most companies, the primary use of social media is content distribution to attract attention and drive website visits. Make sure all your blog posts are distributed through the major social media channels listed below. At a minimum, have a presence and post content on these Websites:

- Facebook
- LinkedIn
- Google+
- Twitter
- YouTube

There are many more social media sites, but these are currently the most important for content to reach the right readers and for SEO purposes. Also, stay on top of the news so you are not caught by surprise when a social media website takes off or disappears.

Google and Social Media

Google appreciates and rewards content activity in social media, especially the big three social media sites, Facebook, LinkedIn and Google+. Google is rewarding companies that establish themselves as content authorities on various subjects with higher placement in search results. This happens over time as you place content online and collect readers in social media websites and through your blog. Look to Google+ as a growing resource in this area and to build your credibility as an author with Google with excellent content all coded for SEO. Also, links to your website from popular social media sites are useful and can't hurt placement in Google search results.

How Much Time Should be Spent on Social Media?

Think of social media as a content and sales tool bringing a return based on the effort put into it. The amount of social media your company needs depends upon your web marketing goals, sales targets and how you are using other web marketing tools. Your web marketing plan should estimate the amount of social media needed based on marketing priorities and your expected return. For most companies, weekly activity and content postings are enough to stay visible and drive traffic. It is important to make sure your company website is in alignment with your web marketing strategy before you spend considerable time on social media sites.

A Complement to Marketing and Sales Efforts

The best use of social media is as a complement to your current sales and marketing efforts. Don't expect too much, but stay active enough to have a presence. Your presence in social media over time will assist in driving traffic to your website, provide content to a wide range of readers and support your brand. Finds ways to use social media as a support to what you already do well in sales and marketing.

Social Media and Selling

Social media websites are very effective selling and prospecting tools, especially LinkedIn. The key is to take part in the conversation, join groups, meet people and network. All the rules of effective selling apply to interactions in social media, but with a much larger prospective audience. Results come when your target market gravitates to the value you provide and become followers, readers and distributers of your content. Your sales team can reach out to these prospects as sales leads.

Remember, your content is very transparent on social media sites. If you are just looking to sell and promote your company, your results will be poor. If you are looking to add value and help others, you can expect a great return.

Social Media and Customer Service Support

For larger companies, social media has also become a support to customer service.

Businesses are watching conversions on social media to help them better service their target market. There are many online tools to help track this content. Because there are not usually enough conversations happening on the social media sites of smaller and medium sized companies, their challenge is to start the conversation to attract attention. This happens when you post valuable content. Don't get too caught up on inappropriate negative content in social media. Focus on adding value and providing a great service or product and look for positive feedback as a result.

Results are Difficult to Measure

Social media results are difficult to measure because most people only read social media posts and do not interact. They may also find out about your company on social media, yet search for your website in

Google. This is why social media stats can be misleading and social media marketing must be seen as a support to SEO efforts and content marketing. You can measure direct traffic to your website from social media in Google Analytics, and social media sites like Facebook and LinkedIn offer the ability to place ads on their sites and offer basic stats programs to review activity from visitors.

SUMMARY

Don't get caught up in social media hype. Be careful to accurately judge the potential of social media for your business and the potential results. Develop a plan based on content marketing and stick to it over the long term. Understand how your target market uses social media and cover the basics as part of your overall web marketing efforts. These steps are the key to a winning formula in social media marketing.

ACTION ITEMS

➤ Include social media in your web marketing and content marketing plan.

➤ Develop a company home page for LinkedIn, Facebook, Google+ and other social media sites as needed for your business.

➤ Track referrals from social media sites to your company website and the number of likes and followers.

➤ Post content weekly to social media sites and link it back to your website.

➤ Post your website blog posts to major social media sites.

➤ Use various forms of content, such as video, photography and other media.

➤ Determine your areas of content expertise and work toward being an online content authority on those subjects. Use social media as an outlet for that content.

➤ As a business leader, visit your company's social media sites on a regular basis to monitor the activity and stay relevant to your content marketing themes.

➤ Keep track of major changes in social media and how the most popular social media sites are used by your target market.

CHAPTER 39

Website Partnerships and Links to Drive Traffic

Google was one of the first search engines to use website popularity as a key indicator of a website's relevance in search results. The Google founders believed websites with more incoming links from other websites should be ranked higher in search results. The more popular the sites linking to your site, the better the search results in Google. This, along with a very simple and easy-to-use home page, contributed to Google's fast growth and eventual dominance in web searches. In fact, Google still remains one of the easiest-to-use search engines, and this has contributed greatly to very high usage and market share dominance.

Inbound links are no longer the primary driver of SEO results in Google. In fact, they have created a huge spam problem for Google, as websites with irrelevant links are found high up in search results. However, links to your site continue to be a significant part of how Google ranks websites in search results, especially if those links are from popular and highly visible sites. Let's review a few key issues to understand when you are working to increase your search results from inbound links.

Build a Relationship to get Links

There are several ways to get links to your website. One of the best is to develop an alliance or partnership with websites in your industry visited by your target market and to request a link exchange. Contact the company directly and make a business or marketing case for the link. Explain how the link will help both companies.

It is also important to establish links from directory and general resource websites. Here are a few suggestions of the types of websites that can provide strong inbound links.

- Industry-related websites
- Association websites
- Industry resource sites such as ThomasNet.com
- Local Yellow Pages websites (YP.com)
- Online directory websites such as Yahoo
- All the major social media sites

For an additional list of directory sites and to get inbound links visit Yext.com. Yext can also provide industry-specific sites and local options.

Avoid Spamming

Collecting inbound links to your website that have no relation to your site is not recommended by Google and may be considered spamming. This approach to inbound links may result in Google penalties. Many SEO companies offer link-building services and they may produce results; however, make sure you build links of value and relevance to your website so your site complies with Google's anti-spamming rules. If you are doing something just to trick Google and drive more traffic, you are running the risk of Google removing your website from their search results. Also, avoid posting to many blog posts, hoping to get inbound links. This is considering spamming by Google.

Multiple Domains and Duplicate Content

Occasionally, web marketers will buy dozens of domain names and build dozens of similar websites, all linking back to the company website. They are looking for more search engine traffic and inbound links. This is a very thin strategy and frowned upon by Google. Building multiple websites, only for the purpose of search engine rankings, may bring a penalty from Google, as they may see duplicate content as a spamming technique. Multiple websites from the same company with unique domains should only be used for unique market segments to meet user needs, not to trick Google into higher search engine rankings.

Track Results in Google Analytics

Links to your site are called referrers in Google Analytics and this is a key metric worth watching. Keep a close eye on the conversions coming from these links. You may find that traffic coming from targeted referring websites through inbound links could have some of the highest conversion rates on your website. This is in addition to the improved search rankings.

SUMMARY

Although it is no longer the major influencer of search rankings for Google, gaining inbound links to your website does help you get a higher position in search results and can generate qualified traffic that converts into a sales leads and sales for your company.

ACTION ITEMS

> Include an inbound link strategy in your web marketing plan.

> Task your marketing team to develop a list of the most popular websites visited by your target market. Reach out to these companies for a link exchange.

> Develop a list of association and directory websites in your marketplace.

> Track inbound links in Google Analytics and in Webmaster Tools.

> Get a link from your website development or ad agency provider to your site.

> Go to Google.com and type in links: followed by your website domain name or links: www.YOURWEBSITE.com and hit enter to see a listing of inbound links pointing to your website in Google's index. This can be done in Webmaster Tools as well.

The Fundamentals of the Mobile Web

The use of mobile devices and a variety of screen sizes to access the Internet is growing fast and will make up a significant portion of visits to your website. In this chapter we will review what business owners and leaders need to know about mobile devices and the Internet and how to position their company to reap marketing benefits from this rapid growth.

Many factors are driving the growth of the mobile Internet, and there is much to consider in understanding this trend. Also, the growth of mobile web is here to stay and bound to change and adapt to more efficient mobile devices such as the iPad and those to come in the future.

Apple Products Lead the Way

In the past two years there has been a surge of website visits from mobile devices. This data is tracked in Google Analytics, and the growth is driven by the iPhone and iPad. These devices have changed how people perceive the Internet from a static interface to something that can go with them anywhere. Certainly, new mobile devices from Apple are helping users to be more comfortable accessing the web away from their desk or office. Yet, there is more to consider in understanding how to market through mobile devices.

Mobile Usage Limits User Options

Users perform very few tasks on their mobile devices and rarely read in-depth online content. They are mostly looking for brief content, an address, phone number or photos with captions. Keep this in mind when designing a mobile website. What are the three most common things your targeted users are doing on your mobile website? How can they easily use their mobile device to contact your company? What content is most important and can be read on the mobile web? Limited user options force web marketers to focus their website's navigation, content and contact information on mobile devices.

Everything is Smaller

Younger people are more likely to use their mobile devices because they have better vision and are not tied to an office or desk. They are more patient with sites not optimized for mobile, but less likely to buy. This is key in understanding that the over-fifty-year-old demographic will need reading glasses to view content on a mobile phone or iPhone. Make it easier on their eyes with larger fonts, graphics and menu items. People with reading glasses have more money to spend online and will appreciate a mobile website that is easy to read and use.

Mobile Devices Indirectly Drive Sales

Very few direct sales will come from an online device. The mobile visit will generally be an opportunity for the user to gather information that will lead to a purchase. Spend less time on helping users buy on your mobile website, and more time making it easy for users to scan your products and services and get in touch with you from their mobile device. Summarize product and service information so it can be read on a smart phone or even smaller screens. A good rule of thumb to follow is larger screen sizes produce more online sales than smaller devices.

Users Want Information Now

The Internet has created an environment where people can get answers to any question immediately. This means it is not OK to not know something! Based on how users navigate mobile websites, it is better for them to contact your company directly for answers. The majority of mobile users only visit one to two web pages on mobile devices. You can meet their needs to get an answer with an easy-to-find e-mail address link or phone number on your mobile website.

The Death of the Traditional Office

Mobile devices enable people to work from any location in their home or workplace. This is leading to fewer personal offices away from home. This trend will continue and also drive the need for mobile devices with larger screens. Where are your targeted mobile users likely to be when researching your company? Are they likely to read your e-mails or website on a mobile device? Look to Google Analytics for answers to these questions.

Responsive Design

Responsive design is currently the most effective website development process for mobile devices and a variety of screen sizes. The second-best option is to build a website with a unique design specifically for mobile devices. Responsive design is preferred because the design elements remain the same as the website automatically adapts itself to various screen sizes and browsers.

Responsive design is an advancement in website technology because the issue in the future will not be whether or not your website can adapt to mobile devices, but whether the website can display effectively on a large variety of screen sizes and types. These screen sizes can be anything from a small screen inside a pair of glasses or a watch, to large projection displays.

What is Unique to Your Target Market?

Determine what is unique to your target market in their use of mobile Internet, and meet those needs on your mobile website. Also, gain understanding of the types and sizes of screens most likely used by your target market to surf the web. Do this right away and be a leader in your field.

SUMMARY

Don't let the surge in mobile website visitors catch you by surprise. Take action and be ready to lead your competitors in this area. Start by understanding how your target market uses mobile devices and a variety of screen sizes to view your website. Don't make assumptions. Go ask them, or better yet, go watch them use mobile devices and check this data in Google Analytics in your monthly web marketing meetings.

ACTION ITEMS

> Identify the top three functions mobile users want from your website.

> Make sure your navigation is simple and use large fonts on your mobile site.

> Conduct market research to get answers about mobile website usage.

> Think about a mobile app as a solution for smart phone users.

> Check out your competitors' websites on a smart phone or other mobile device.

> Consider responsive design as an option for your website so the site is able to modify itself for each individual user's screen size.

> Track mobile visits to your website in Google Analytics. If your mobile traffic is approaching 15-20 percent of your overall visits, it is time to invest in a mobile website or a responsive design website.

CHAPTER 41

STEP FOUR: Monitoring ROI and Tracking Results

The fourth step of the Four-Step Process is perhaps the most important. It is the glue holding the process together and drives results and accountability for web marketing action plans. The final step brings the first three together and is used to receive and update the action items in the first three steps. This involves a process for tracking web marketing results in your web stats, meetings to review web marketing efforts, online conversions and a method for tracking ROI. From this step will come modifications to the web marketing strategies and action plans to improve conversions and drive a strong, measurable ROI. Step four sets the web marketing priorities for your team based on clear data and feedback from website users.

Action Items are the Key Value of Step Four

It may be that you'll start with the action items in step four and use them to update your strategy, which in turn leads to website updates and traffic generation updates. Any way you look at it, step four is critical to success because it drives the review and analysis that brings about action plans to improve the first three steps. The action items in step four are composed of the daily and weekly web marketing work used to improve results. Most of the web marketing team's time will be spent in step four activities.

Web Marketing Needs Constant Attention

Don't take step four lightly because it is the final step in the process. Many web marketers spend less time on step four than they should. This is especially true after they redesign and launch a new website. Websites are not like printed brochures which are completed when sent to print. Websites must be constantly updated with fresh content. They are always changing and adapting to better meet visitor needs and those needs change over time.

The Power of Regular Web Marketing Meetings

Just like sales and marketing teams meet regularly to review strategies and action plans, so should web marketers. These web marketing meetings should be focused solely on website data and action items needed to improve website results. They should also coordinate with the company's sales and marketing teams.

Analytics to Measure Sales and ROI

At the core of step four is gathering the data needed to track conversion results and measure ROI. Web stats become the direction for step four action items, and the proper interpretation of web data can have a tremendous impact on business results. We will now go deeper into step four so you can learn how to evaluate the proper web data in order to deliver excellent returns on investment from your web marketing efforts.

CHAPTER 42

Monitoring ROI in Web Marketing

Before we dive into step four, let's review the Four-Step Process once again. They are:

- Web marketing strategy

- Website design and development

- Traffic generation

- Conversion tracking and return on investment (ROI)

In this chapter, we will discuss the importance of tracking web marketing ROI. Most small companies are notorious for not tracking the ROI behind sales and marketing functions. They tend to wing it and rely too much on anecdotal information when reviewing sales efforts. Web marketing is data driven and removes the blind guesses that often result from the lack of quantifiable sales data and reporting. The first step in determining ROI is establishing the necessary tracking analytics and processes.

Track Web Marketing ROI with Google Analytics and Webmaster Tools

All that you have learned in this book can become irrelevant very quickly if there is not a process for tracking results for each strategy and tactic. Thankfully, there are two great Google tools to help you track the Four-Step Process: Google Analytics and Webmaster Tools are central to step four. These are incredibly useful, free web site statistical tools provided by Google to make tracking ROI easy.

The challenge becomes establishing the infrastructure and company culture for reviewing web data and tracking results on a regular basis. The best method for dealing with this challenge is to hold regular web marketing meetings with your team. From these meetings will come action items followed by modifications to your web marketing strategy to improve ROI and reach your targets. Your web marketing goals set the bar for the meeting agenda and quantify your success levels.

How to Set Web Marketing Goals

Google Analytics reports on hundreds of web statistics and variations. It can seem overwhelming at first. Yet, understanding which stats are most important and how to interpret those stats are the first steps in setting web marketing goals. Let's start with an overview of the most important web stats to track and a review of how to set goals in each key area.

Here are the key stats to watch:

Website Visitors

This can be measured by total visits, unique visits, new visitors and repeat visits. Your site should target about 75 percent of total visits from new visitors. Critical mass for websites is usually reached when traffic volumes approach a minimum of 1,500 to 2,000 visits per month. This is the most important web stat to follow closely, and it's a key business indicator for your company. Review website visits weekly, if possible.

Pages per Visit and Time on Site

This is an indication of interest and website engagement. Target as goals four to five pages per visit and three minutes on the site. This will drive a healthy conversion rate.

Bounce Rate

The bounce rate is a measurement of visitors leaving immediately, or bouncing off your website, versus going deeper into the site and visiting more than one page. A bounce rate of 25 percent means that 25 percent of your website visitors leave after visiting only one page. Target a bounce rate below 40 percent for lead generation websites and 30 percent or below for e-commerce sites.

Traffic Sources

- There are three basic sources of website traffic:

- Search engine traffic (organic and paid)

- Links from other websites

- Direct traffic

Set a goal of 50 percent of your traffic coming from organic search engine results and 25 percent or more coming from links from other websites. Direct traffic is good, but does not usually represent business growth from new site visitors. Most direct traffic comes from people that already know your company.

Online Conversions

Online conversions are inquiries or sales generated from your website. Target 1 to 2 percent conversion rates for lead generation efforts and 2 to 5 percent conversion rates for e-commerce websites. See the upcoming chapter on conversions to learn more.

Sales Conversion and Average Order Amount

How good is your sales team at closing sales? What percentage of sales leads does the team convert into sales? What is your average order amount for closed sales? These two numbers are important parts of the ROI equation and will drive your return from web marketing investments.

There are many more stats and data points in Google Analytics; however, these are the most important. Benchmarks and targets should be set in each area and reviewed in your monthly web marketing meetings.

Schedule Web Marketing Meetings

Regularly scheduled web marketing meetings provide the fuel and accountability to drive web marketing ROI. At a minimum, schedule a monthly meeting to review website data and action plans. These meetings force the team to review data and develop action items that drive attention to the web marketing efforts and measuring ROI. The team should focus on reaching website goals as seen in Google Analytics data. It is the day-in and day-out work on improving these stats that drives sales growth.

Here is a typical agenda for an effective web marketing meeting:

- Web stats review and analysis

- Review of goals and forecasted ROI

- Competitive website review

- Usability and conversion analysis

- Design and development updates

- Traffic generation SEO and social media

- Content marketing

- Monthly action items

The simple act of setting a meeting and reviewing this data will help drive web marketing ROI and also train you and the team to be more effective web marketers.

ACTION ITEMS

➤ Establish a Google Analytic and Webmaster Tools account for tracking data on your website.

➤ Set goals for your Google Analytics stats and calculate ROI from those goals.

➤ Schedule monthly web marketing meetings to review this data.

➤ Assign action items to team members and review outcomes in the monthly meetings. Update and review all action items during the meetings.

➤ Determine your sales team's closing ratios and your average order amount.

➤ Review in more detail the conversion and ROI worksheets in the later chapters of this book.

CHAPTER 43

What Business Leaders Need to Know About Google Analytics

Google Analytics is the Internet's leading website statistic monitoring program. It is provided free by Google so web marketers can use the data to measure results from Google AdWords and so Google can watch web data from millions of websites. This has worked very well for Google, now one of the world's most successful and valuable companies. In return, Google Analytics has become a valuable resource and a key business and marketing indicator for many companies. Google believes that once web marketers can see the data, they will work to get more traffic to their website through AdWords, which provides revenues for Google.

Google Analytics as a Key Performance Indicator

The Google Analytics data tracked from your website is a key marketing indicator, and will help you understand market share, how your brand is interpreted, the composition of your target market segments and much more. Business leaders should review this data on a regular basis and compare it to other key indicators. Just reviewing the data and asking questions is extremely valuable. Here are a few of the most important Google Analytics stats to keep an eye on.

- Unique visits

- Bounce rate

- Pages per visit and time on the site

- Traffic sources

- Content visits

- Mobile visits

Conversion Monitoring

As was mentioned in the previous chapter, set goals for each of these key stats. Don't make the mistake of turning these reports over to your IT department or others on your team to analyze, without reviewing and understanding the data yourself as the business leader. This information will help you make better decisions and drive marketing results, as the reports are the guideposts for the success of the web marketing strategy. You can bet your competitors are watching this data on their website.

Google Analytics as a Leading Indicator

Google Analytics data is a leading indicator and can help you see trends in your business before they impact your bottom line. Google Analytics is a great tool for monitoring market share based on website visits and conversions. Because of the growth of pull marketing, where prospective customers research in anonymity on the Internet before making contact, it is possible for companies to experience market share losses and not know it is happening until it impacts revenue. Watching your web stats allows you to see these trends and modify your marketing strategy as needed.

The best and most straightforward way to see the date from Google Analytics as a leading performance indicator is to think about website visitor trends. In most cases, traffic increases to your website are an indicator sales are growing and traffic declines indicate a loss of potential customers. (Of course, seasonal variations and one-time events can impact these trends.)

Google Analytics is a leading indicator in many areas, including the content preferences of your target market, use of mobile devices, links from other websites and much more. A well-informed and strategic business leader will include website data in key indicator reports.

Google Webmaster Tools

Google Webmaster Tools is an essential part of your search engine optimization (SEO) work and should be linked to Google Analytics as a key tracking tool. The focus of Webmaster Tools is SEO and getting found in Google search results. Webmaster Tools is important for Google in their goal of preventing spam websites from being found in their search results. It is important for web marketers so they can see the keyword phrases used to pull up their website in Google. As of this writing, much of this keyword data is being blocked in Google Analytics. It appears that Google does not want to provide the information for free and would rather have web marketers use their Google AdWords program to see search impressions and gather keyword data. Webmaster Tools allows you to see the communications between your website and the Google search engine. Webmaster Tools and Google Analytics are two of the most important online tools needed to drive results from web marketing.

SUMMARY

Most business leaders do not regularly review their web stats and this is a mistake. It can lead to poor decision making and an inability to notice market share losses or other key business trends as they are happening in real time. For example, a significant increase or drop in website traffic will impact company sales. This data is easily found in Google Analytics along with much more valuable company information. Make the time to review your website stats and learn how to act on this valuable, free data coming from Google.

ACTION ITEMS

> Review Google Analytics data from your website on a weekly or monthly basis.

> If needed, have these reports e-mailed to you or printed and on your desk.

> If possible, attend web marketing meetings with your sales and marketing staff on a regular basis and ask questions about Google Analytics stats.

> Link Google Analytics to Webmaster Tools and AdWords.

> Develop Google Analytics into a leading indicator for your business.

> Ask questions about trends seen in your web data and use the information to make better strategic marketing decisions for your company.

CHAPTER 44

Web Marketing Stats and Benchmarks

We have reviewed the importance of monitoring web stats and their impact on sales revenues and ROI. Setting realistic benchmarks and targets to help accurately measure results is critical to online marketing success. The best web stat of all is an online conversion in the form of a lead for your sales team or an online order.

Using the information in the previous chapter, you should have an idea of the number of conversions you can expect from your website, given the amount of traffic visiting the site. This is where a conversion strategy can make a big difference in your web marketing results. Start the process of setting your goals and benchmarks by clearly defining your conversion strategy using the following steps:

- Set up Google Analytics and Webmaster Tools.

- Establish a conversion strategy in your web marketing plan defining how online conversions happen and what will motivate a website visitor to convert.

- Make a list of all the various types of online conversions within this strategic approach. (More on this subject in coming chapters).

- Include effective calls to action and conversion points in the strategy.

- Schedule web marketing meetings to develop action plans based on website data and reports.

After these foundational items are in place, you can begin thinking about setting targets for your web marketing goals and benchmarks as reviewing in Google Analytics and Webmaster Tools.

Web Marketing Targets

Here are the most important web marketing targets and benchmarks to establish and monitor. The targets will vary based on the size of your company and current web strategy.

- **Unique Visitors** – Target a minimum of 1,500 unique visitors per month with growth of about 20 percent per year. Website data becomes more useful as you increase website visits. A target of 2,000 or more website visitors per month is ideal.

- **Page Views per Visitor** – The number of pages viewed per visit should be at least four to five on average. This is a measurement of engagement with the site's content and sites with fewer page views per visitor have fewer conversions.

- **Time on Website** – This is also a measurement of the visitor's engagement with the website and should average at least three minutes.

- **Bounce Rate** – The bounce rate is a very important benchmark that should be below 40 percent for content-based lead generation websites and below 30 percent for e-commerce websites. The bounce rate is the percentage of website visitors that "bounce" off the website quickly and only visit one page, usually the home page.

- **Traffic Sources** – Traffic sources comprise three key areas. The first is search engine traffic, which should be over 50 percent of your site's total visits. The second is direct traffic or visitors that know your website domain name and go directly to your site. The third is web traffic from other websites that link to your site.

- **Blog Postings** – Content should be posted to your blog on a weekly basis and the blog should be one of the top ten most visited sections on the site.

- **Social Media Postings** – Blog postings and other social media content should be posted weekly and visits to social media sites should also be tracked, along with interactions from social media to your website.

- **Lead Conversion Rate** – Target a conversion rate of 1 to 3 percent of total visits becoming sales leads for a lead generation, content-based website.

- **Online Sales Conversion Rate** – Target a conversion rate of 3 to 5 percent for e-commerce websites selling products online.

- **Shopping Cart Abandonment** – Set a target of less than 50 percent for e-commerce shopping cart abandonment rates. This means less than half of the people that complete a shopping cart should drop out of the process before they purchase.

- **Average Order Amount** – This applies to e-commerce websites and should be over $100 per order if possible. This stat should also be tracked for lead generation sites, as it will impact ROI calculations.

Extend Web Targets into the Sales Process

These targets should be reviewed and compared with your sales team's benchmarks. All of these targets work together to measure sales and marketing effectiveness and to drive sales revenues. A key conversion point for the sales team is the ratio of web leads that turn into customers. Another key factor in this conversion rate is the length of time customers stay with the company. Both of those benchmarks are related to your web marketing efforts and the quality of your leads. The quality of your website visitor is a result of your website marketing strategy.

SUMMARY

Use the key points in this chapter to set clear web marketing goals and specific targets from your web stats. It will be a challenge to grow sales through your Internet marketing efforts if you are not clear on web marketing goals. These goals also become discussion points in your web marketing meetings and guideposts in reviewing your website stats.

ACTION ITEMS

➤ Set up Google Analytics and Webmaster Tools.

➤ Set targets for each key web stat mentioned in this chapter.

➤ Prepare a written report for the entire sales and marketing team including these benchmarks.

➤ Review goals at the beginning of your monthly web marketing meetings.

➤ Set action plans that relate to improvements for each web marketing goal.

➤ Set online growth targets and goal improvements for each month and year.

Develop Conversion Strategies to Drive Growth

The goal of this book, and the objective of your web marketing action plans, are increased sales revenues for your company. The sales process starts with an online conversion. Sales growth is driven by various forms of website conversions and your web marketing strategies must be tied to a conversion path or target. In part, website conversions are defined as any contact or interaction from a website visitor to your company generated from your web marketing efforts.

There are many ways to set and monitor website conversions. This includes the process of moving your website visitors toward contact with your company. This is the online sales funnel, and Google Analytics can be used to monitor the steps users take along this path. The user path along the online sales funnel may not be a direct contact, but should be a step in the right direction toward contact with your company.

Website Conversion Funnel

It is important to structure your website navigation and content as if it were a sales funnel. This is the natural progression the average web visitor takes as they move toward a conversion. For example, a website visitor will first start at the home page and determine what your company is about and where they can find value. From there they will gravitate to more information about the company or your products and services. At this point, some users will dig deeper for more detailed content as they do their research. Others will gravitate toward their preferred conversion method following this content review. Tracking the sales funnel in Google Analytics will provide insights into how to increase conversion rates. The online sales funnel often begins with various content pages and usually ends at your website's Contact Us page.

The Contact Us Page

The Contact Us page is one of the most important pages on your website. Its goal is to drive visitor contacts and should be included in your main navigation menu. The Contact Us page must include various contact methods because website visitors have different preferences for getting in touch with your company. Include the following contact methods and information on your Contact Us page.

- Website dedicated phone and fax numbers
- Address and locations
- Driving instructions
- Office hours
- Web submission form
- E-mail contact information

Communicate to website visitors that you want to hear from them, and let visitors know how long it takes to get a response back from your company. Website visitors appreciate a quick turnaround from their inquiries and quick responses lead to higher close rates when selling to these prospects. Also, include contact information on every page of your website in the footer or header.

Calls to Action

Website "calls to action" (sometimes called CTAs) lead people toward a conversion point. Be creative, as there are no limitations on the types of conversions you can establish and track online. The better you understand how website visitors prefer to contact you and what motivates them to make contact, the better your conversion rates.

Should website visitors have to sign up as a call to action before you send them more information or content? It depends, but it is not usually a good idea, because users don't like it. Test variations and see what happens. Be generous with your content. You will see results and more conversions and if you don't provide this content, your competitors will.

In addition to the contact methods found on your website's Contact Us page, include these key conversion points on your website and in social media.

- E-mail newsletter sign up
- Blog and content RSS feeds

- Share buttons for social media and e-mail
- Free downloads of specialty content or white papers
- Call to action buttons for special offers
- Likes and follows in social media

Website Submission Forms

Always include a website submission form on your site. Keep in mind that shorter forms get more conversions and longer forms get fewer conversions, but tend to better qualify the sales lead. Visitors often prefer forms because they may not be able to easily e-mail from their computer or device and they may be researching your business after hours and no one is available to take a phone call. Also, forms are easily tracked in Google Analytics and are generally excellent online conversion methods. Respond quickly to form requests so you can maximize your conversion rate and close more sales.

Tips to Generate More Website Conversions

Here are a few ideas for generating more conversions from your website:

- Website visitors are impulsive, so keep content scannable and links simple.

- Set the right message and call to action in your content.

- Place calls to action near popular content and on every page.

- Allow for more depth of content for analytical people.

- The shopping cart must be first rate, easy to use and intuitive.

- Use color photos with captions.

- Avoid objects that look like ads or large graphics. Online advertising is a turn-off.

- Customize landing pages for unique web search terms.

- Content and knowledge drives conversions, not flash and graphics.

- Product photos on all pages and detailed descriptions are very important.

- If possible, offer a money back guarantee.

- Call your website the official website for your company.

- Use unique web phone numbers on every page.

- Test special offers and incentives, especially free shipping.

- Is the motive of the website to sell stuff or help people? Make the site's purpose to help people.

- Draw qualified traffic from the search engines.

- Have a professional, high-quality design.

- Use consistent branding and messaging on the site.

- Be very well-organized in navigation and usability, as this builds credibility.

- Load the website with content and media that excites visitors.

- Use a compelling offer that moves people to action.

SUMMARY

Website conversions, in their most basic form, can be defined as either a direct sale via e-commerce or the generation of a sales lead. These are the two most common forms of online conversions. People that buy from your company or make contact in any way should fall into comprehensive stay-in-touch program. Remember, solid conversion rates come from a strategic process, great content, an excellent understanding of your users and solid web marketing planning.

ACTION ITEMS

➤ Make sure there is a link to your Contact Us page in your main navigation and that it is present on all web pages.

➤ Include various call to action buttons on your web pages and understand your site visitors' preference for conversions.

➤ Set up conversion tracking in Google Analytics and in AdWords to track ROI.

➤ Establish a conversion rate goal of 1 percent or more of total website traffic.

➤ Monitor which type of website traffic converts, and build on that data to refine your web marketing strategies.

➤ Review your competitors' conversion points and make use of best practices.

➤ Test several conversion options to determine what types of conversions work best.

➤ Include spam prevention methods on your contact forms and e-mail addresses.

CHAPTER 46

Conversion Types and Stay-in-Touch Programs

Getting an online conversion is a big accomplishment. It says a lot about your website's content, usability, branding and your web marketing efforts in general. People don't convert unless there is real intent, and even the best websites only convert a small fraction of website visitors. However, getting the conversion is only the starting point to increasing sales revenues. More has to happen for online conversions to grow sales over the long-term. The key objective is for an online conversion to be the first step toward a sale or an ongoing customer relationship through a well-established stay-in-touch program.

Stay-in-touch programs are the methods used by your company to remain in contact with your target market, sales prospects, loyal followers of your content, and customers. These programs come in many forms and will be reviewed in more detail later in this chapter.

Let's start with a more detailed review of the various types of online conversions and a few strategies for an effective stay-in-touch program. We will begin by gaining a better understanding of your site's visitors.

Get Inside the Head of Website Visitors

It is a big step for website visitors to move from the anonymity of reviewing a website to actually contacting your company. Website users are moved to action when the content on a website motivates them to get more information or buy. This usually happens after several websites are visited, researched and your website content wins them over. If your website does its job, it will be easy for web leads to understand why you are better than your competitors. Website visitors have done their homework and want to be taken seriously. Because of this, a web lead is a very important lead.

The better you understand the intentions of the website visitor, the better your site will convert new customers. Don't guess at this or wing it—get real data from your web stats and through market research with your target markets. You will find in your research that website users like options and have various preferences for making contact with your company.

Website Visitors Prefer Conversion Options

It is important to note that web users do not care if you know how they contacted your company, and they prefer a variety of contact methods. The boundary of how people convert can be very blurry at times, especially if they call your office or do not reach out to you online. This can make tracking conversions difficult. Therefore, a variety of conversion points can help drive leads and sales. This insures your site is meeting the needs of ten out of ten site visitors.

Here is a summary of several online conversion points preferred by a variety of users:

Direct Online Sale

- Telephone sale or inquiry
- Call to support or customer service
- E-mail inquiry
- Contact form submission
- Blog RSS subscription
- E-mail newsletter subscription
- Social media follow or like
- Refer a friend
- App download (with no purchase)
- Podcast subscription
- Webinar or seminar registration
- PDF or other download
- Security, privacy and return policy statements
- Testimonials, case studies and reviews
- Shipping information
- Usability of the Contact Us page and checkout process

Multiple conversion points help grow your stay-in-touch program and better market your website and company by meeting user needs. Find those that work best for your website and track the results.

THE ONLINE CONVERSION PROCESS

The online conversion process can be broken down into a seven point process. Each of these seven areas must be addressed in your web marketing plan and included in your website design process. These are the ingredients of a successful online conversion process to drive sales growth.

1. **Online Content** – The content preferred by your target market is the most common entry point for your website and the conversion process. The content on your website will attract the visitor to you and motivate them to contact your company. The term "content marketing" best describes this process and is a key to your conversion process. We have devoted chapter 36 in this book to content marketing and its impact on traffic generation and sales.

   Review the content marketing chapter for more details as your website content is the starting point for any online conversion.

2. **The Offer** – This is the specific piece of content that drives interest from website visitors and moves them to a call to action or contact with your company.

3. **Call to Action** – Your call to action is the conversion point where the user takes action. This could be an online form, e-mail address, phone number or other conversion point. A complete list of conversion points are included above.

4. **Web Landing Page** – This is the landing page where the user reads more about the call to action and completes a form or gets a phone number. There is an art and science to landing page development to drive conversions. Keep this page simple and test various offers.

5. **The Submission Form** – Short submission forms asking for basic information get higher conversion rates. Longer forms qualify better, but have lower completion rates. All websites must have submission forms on the Contact Us page and throughout the website.

6. **Contact with the Sales Team** – The sales team receives the contact information, begins the follow-up process and ensures the lead is also added to the company's stay-in-touch program and customer relationship management (CRM) system. Respond promptly to leads from your website.

7. **Stay-in-Touch Program** – The sales team should remain in contact with all leads generated from online marketing and add those leads to the company's stay-in-touch program.

Conversions and the Stay-in-Touch Program

The success of online conversion programs is only as good as your stay-in-touch program. Your stay-in-touch program is what you do to remain in contact with your target market after the lead or sales conversion. Develop a strategy for keeping in touch and allow for multiple channels. Here are a few ways to keep in touch with your target market after the initial connection is made with the prospective customer.

- E-mail marketing
- Webinars
- Social media content postings
- Blogs and RSS feeds
- Podcasts
- Website content updates
- Direct mail
- Phone calls and CRM systems
- Calls to action and incentives
- Face-to-face meetings

The key to successful stay-in-touch programs is strong content and a solid content distribution strategy to make sure you remain in touch with web leads. These programs are very powerful and should be very cost effective with an excellent ROI.

E-mail as a Stay-in-Touch Program

E-mail marketing is one of the most effective stay-in-touch methods. It is cost effective and can drive sales with valuable content for readers. You may have to contact leads several times before they buy, and some may take a few months to become customers. Use an e-mail stay-in-touch program to follow up with web leads. This is especially important because if you market well online, your web-based leads will soon overwhelm your budget and ability to follow up properly in person. Write valuable e-mail content. Important e-mails are read and sent to others. Junk e-mail gets deleted. Your e-mail content should never be considered spam or "junk" by your target market!

All web-based leads should go into the stay-in-touch e-mail program and e-mail marketing will most likely be the most commonly used stay-in-touch program.

The Bottom Line is Effective ROI

Stay-in-touch automation is a critical part of your sales funnel and allows you to reach an unlimited amount of people. It puts the prospect in charge of the sales process as they contact you when they are ready to buy. These factors work together to drive excellent ROI.

Web marketing budgets are dropping fast as marketing automation and use of technology greatly lowers overall marketing costs. E-mail marketing and blog RSS feeds are two highly cost-effective ways to keep in touch with web-based leads and followers.

Here are a few ROI tips that work in conjunction with your content conversion strategies and your stay-in-touch programs.

* Avoid proprietary technology for your website.

* The CEO and business leaders must understand Google Analytics and use it as a key business indicator to measure ROI.

* Set up and use Google Webmaster Tools with Google Analytics.

* Know which web stats to watch closely and which to ignore.

* Get feedback from market research and usability testing.

* Use automation and technology to maximize your content reach.

* Conduct a review of CRM tools such as SalesForce.com and Basecamp.

* Develop comprehensive marketing analytics based on the marketing funnel and conversion tracking.

How the Sales Team Should Handle a Web Lead

The first contact with a web lead will often be from your sales team. It is very important the sales and marketing team understands how to deal with web leads and knows when to continue selling and when to place the lead in the stay-in-touch program. This also has a major impact on conversion rates and ROI.

The biggest mistake sales teams make is to discount the importance of a web lead or prospect. Web leads are very different from traditional leads because they have already done their homework and researched your offerings. Traditional sales leads, who do not research online, may take more sales time and are usually not as prepared. A sales lead is not necessarily a better qualified prospect because they take more time. Sales teams should spend more time listening and understanding the web-based prospect and less time explaining what the prospect has already read or seen on your website. This can shorten your sales cycle and save the company time and money.

The second biggest mistake companies make with web leads is not having a structure or method for dealing with leads or follow-up to online sales. Salespeople should be reporting on the status of web leads and your website stats should be tracking all conversions. Sales management should know the time it takes to get back to web leads and the process for follow-up with web leads. Make sure your sales team is trained to effectively manage leads from the website and to take these leads seriously.

The faster your sales team can respond to a web-based lead, the more trust is built in the firm and the higher the chances of closing. Respond immediately for better results. Web users appreciate this and you can catch them with your company fresh on their mind. In fact, web-based software even allows you to respond to web leads while they are still on your website!

Questions to Ask the Sales and Marketing Team

Here are a few questions to ask your sales team about how web leads are handled:

- What is our strategy for handling website leads?

- What is the average length of time to respond to a web lead?

- What are the steps in converting web leads?

- What is our conversion rate on web leads?

- Where do web leads fit in our sales process?

- How do you follow up with leads and sales from the web?

- What content areas and pages on the website generate leads?

- Can we use live chat on the website?

- What happens after the sale is closed from our website?

Asking your sales and marketing managers these questions will lead to action items that improve their process and greater success with web leads.

SUMMARY

Develop an action plan around getting online conversions and dropping those lead conversions into a strong stay-in-touch program, leveraging technology to save time and money. This can drive sales growth and ROI levels that can be the most profitable of all your web marketing expenses.

ACTION ITEMS

➤ Research the conversion methods preferred by your target market.

➤ Outline your conversion strategy from the seven items listed in this chapter.

➤ Write a strategic stay-in-touch program as part of your web marketing plan.

➤ Include a budget (time or money) and ROI analysis for your stay-in-touch program.

➤ Select the stay-in-touch channels that work for your target market.

➤ Develop content and call-to-action themes to build your e-mail list.

➤ Post all stay-in-touch content to your website and code it for SEO.

➤ Talk to your target market for feedback on how they want you to stay in touch.

➤ Coordinate the conversion and stay-in-touch process with your sales team.

CHAPTER 47

How to Run a Web Marketing Meeting

This book has made strong arguments for the importance of effective web marketing, the growth of pull marketing and the ability to measure ROI from online marketing efforts. Yet, most companies fail to give web marketing the proper attention by reviewing their web stats or developing ongoing action plans to improve web marketing results. One of the best things an organization can do to stop this pattern is to schedule monthly web marketing meetings.

Just the act of scheduling the web marketing meeting moves the team in the right direction and will put in place the mechanisms needed to track online marketing results. Holding the monthly meeting keeps people accountable regarding completing web marketing action items and reviewing web stats and data. Each action item and website statistic can be reviewed for its impact on web marketing targets and ROI. It also forces the team to learn and understand more about the meaning behind the web stats.

Who Should Attend the Meeting?

The web marketing team should be made up of a variety of individuals with a variety of skill sets. This includes designers, technology staff, photographers, content writers, SEO specialists and more. For the most part, web marketing meetings should be attended by the key decision makers involved in running web marketing programs. This would include the web marketing director, traffic generation staff and project managers. See chapter 16 for more detail on the make-up of your web marketing team.

Design and technology team members can be brought in to these meetings on occasion, but they are not necessarily the focal point of the meetings, nor should they lead the meeting. Many business leaders make the mistake of spending too much time on technology and design issues, because the meetings are generally driven by designers and IT developers. Develop action plans in the meetings to provide direction for graphic designers and IT team members and use the meeting time to review strategy and major action items.

Action Items and Accountability

Each meeting should include a review of your online marketing goals and targets. This includes a review of web stats from Google Analytics, Webmaster Tools, SEO reports and other data. The stats review should highlight the areas where online marketing efforts are excelling and where there is room for improvement as measured in your web marketing targets and goals.

Sample Web Marketing Meeting Agenda

Here are common areas to include in a typical agenda for an effective web marketing meeting.

- **Web Stats Review** – This is an analysis of Google Analytics, Webmaster Tools, AdWords reports and other SEO and web marketing reports. Work with monthly data and compare year-to-date stats against the prior year and the monthly goals set for your website.

- **Goals, Targets and ROI** – If you don't already have goals, then set them before your first meeting and review your targets as they relate to your web strategy.

- **Competitive Website Reviews** – Many competitor websites and online marketing strategies have excellent best practices you can learn from and improve upon. Review competitor websites in your meetings and find best practices that can work for your website.

- **Usability and Conversion Analysis** – This is a review of what works on the site to drive sales conversions. Website usability impacts online conversions and the meeting is a good time to discuss and review the site's usability and user testing. There could be an issue in the area of web usability if your website conversion goals are not meeting targets.

- **Design and Development Updates** – This should be discussed in each meeting as it can improve the company's branding, website usability and overall conversion rates. Include feedback from website users in these discussions. Website design is never completed and can always be improved. Web stats shed light on the effectiveness of your design.

- **Online Traffic Generation** – This discussion is mostly composed of increasing visitor traffic through SEO, new content, social media and links from referring websites. This is an ongoing project that is never complete and is measured very closely in your web stats.

- **Content Marketing Updates** – Content drives both traffic and conversions and the web marketing meeting is a good place to review online content results. Use the meeting to determine which content is most popular among site users and develop action plans to add new blog posts to the site and other content that can help attract visitors to your website and motivate them to contact your company.

- **Monthly Action Items** – Action items, team member accountability and due dates are critical to web marketing success. Assign a project manager to see action items are completed. This final agenda item is the reason for the meeting, and without it meetings can be a waste of time and drain your budget.

SUMMARY

Web marketing meetings should be scheduled to review strategies and develop action plans to drive marketing and sales results. Inbound marketing from your website is important enough to warrant these meetings on a regular basis, either weekly or monthly at a minimum.

ACTION ITEMS

➤ Schedule monthly web marketing meetings for the next twelve months.

➤ Use the agenda in this chapter and ask team members to come prepared to review each area.

➤ Budget about sixty to ninety minutes for the meeting and close with a review of action items with assigned team members and due dates. Your first meetings will take more time and the meetings will become more streamlined over time.

➤ Set criteria and targets for action items.

➤ Be prepared to answer questions about web marketing data in each meeting.

➤ Leave each meeting with a clear action plan to improve web marketing results.

CHAPTER 48

How to Modify Your Web Strategy

One of the biggest mistakes made by business leaders is thinking their website strategy or design is complete and does not need ongoing attention after the site goes live. You may not need to overhaul web strategy in each web marketing meeting, but you do need to react to the data from your web stats and constantly be finding ways to improve results and modify the strategy. These strategy modification efforts are key to increasing website traffic and maximizing conversion rates.

The driving factor behind step four of the Four-Step Process is the ability to successfully modify a business web marketing strategy based on the available web stats and feedback from your site's visitors. This is usually done in the team's web marketing meetings and implemented through the team's action plans generated as a result of these meetings.

How Often to Update the Home Page and Key Taglines

For the most part, your home page design does not need to change very often. However, after two to three years the design will be stale and will need an update to look fresh and current. Work with your designer on this process and observe design trends among your competitor websites and other sites you frequent online.

The content focus and key messaging on your home page should be updated more frequently. What are the most important things happening at your company that you want website visitors to know about? This should be updated monthly or even weekly. We don't recommend a "what's new" section because few people click on those pages and most companies are not able to keep this section current. Rather, place new home page content in a brief tagline in your main banner or just below the banner or home page images. Your website home page is usually the most popular web page on your site and is a great place for content updates about your company.

It is important to note that Internet users are becoming very keen to the look of a website's home page. They will know if you have an old design or if your design is fresh and up to date. Older looking websites do not communicate a strong brand, especially to younger site visitors who have grown up with the Internet. This is another reason to make regular design updates and keep the site fresh and modern looking.

When to Change the Focus of Website Content

As we discussed in previous chapters, content is critical to your website's success and you must have a plan for regular content updates through your blog and in other content areas on the website. You may find a need to change the focus of your content if your stats do not show strong user engagement. For example, if your web pages have bounce rates over 50 percent, less than three pages per visit, or low time per page visit, these are indicators your content is not appealing to readers. This would be a good time to reach out to a few people in your target market for feedback on the type of content with higher value for website visitors. Higher value content drives more traffic and conversions and all this is measured in your web stats.

The most active content area of your website will be the company blog. However, new product and service areas should be updated as needed and highlighted in your main navigation menu.

When to Update Website Navigation

The effectiveness of your website navigation is also measured in your web stats. Your site should include a well-thought-out navigation menu and site map that is intuitive to users with easy-to-understand link titles. You should see a fairly even distribution of visits among the website's pages. If you find that a handful of pages are dominating user time, then your navigation may be making it difficult for users to access multiple web pages. You may need to consolidate web pages and possibly simplify the navigation structure. Remember, website navigation is one of the most important parts of your website and can make or break your web marketing goals.

Search Engine Landing Pages

Review your web stats for key search engine landing pages on your site and check user engagement on those pages. These are the first web pages visited by website users. They are driving visits from Google and are important entry points to your website. Google has indexed these pages in their search engine and they are very important to your web strategy and driving results because they are a key branding point for your company in addition to the home page. You can never change the first impression of your company website, and often that first impression does not come from your home page, but from an interior landing page. All this data is measured in your web stats.

Promotions, Special Offers and Incentives

These marketing action items are an ongoing part of your web strategy implementation and it is best to use what has worked offline and to also test various approaches to drive results. Any promotion or special incentive should be tracked in your web data and measured in your conversion tracking. This will take out the guess work in determining what works best for your business to incentivize sales growth. If promotions are a part of your marketing plan, then include them in your web marketing meetings and update your website accordingly. Make sure to coordinate your offline efforts with your online marketing.

SUMMARY

Website data is the key indicator and driver of strategy updates and modifications. If something is working on the website and meeting your expectations, then keep doing what is working. However, when the web stats report problem areas for your website, take time to modify your web strategy to improve results. This all starts by scheduling web marketing meetings and reviewing web stats on a regular basis. Make website improvements with new content and information to keep visitors engaged and conversion rates optimized as a part of your web marketing culture.

ACTION ITEMS

> ➤ Look for red flags in your website data that drive strategy updates and modifications to your website.

> ➤ Make this a part of your web marketing meetings and your marketing culture so that your website is constantly improving.

> ➤ Review your home page weekly and develop a plan for regular updates.

> ➤ Check your web stats to determine the landing pages or entry points for website visitors other than the home page.

> ➤ Include website usability improvements as part of your site's regular updates and reach out to your current and prospective customers for feedback.

> ➤ Understand that your website is always under construction.

CHAPTER 49

Web Marketing ROI Worksheets

We have discussed in great detail the importance of web marketing ROI and how it connects to a successful online marketing strategy. In this chapter, we will provide ROI examples and a system for tracking the ROI from website marketing. Tracking ROI is a necessary part of a successful web marketing strategy. This is easily done, thanks to Google Analytics and other web data tracking tools.

It is important to develop a method to accurately calculate ROI. Below are two ROI examples following a proven method based on the Four-Step Process. This method can be applied to your company using your web stats and data from your sales team. You may think this tracking is common sense and used by most companies. However, most businesses do not track web marketing ROI or have a process for accurately measuring online results.

The first example is ROI tracking from a typical lead generation website.

ROI TRACKING: Lead Generation Websites

The majority of websites on the Internet are looking to generate leads for the sales team based, for the most part, on static website content. Here are the key components, with sample dollar amounts and conversion rates included, of ROI calculations for lead generation websites. You will need this information to accurately track the ROI from your company's lead generation site.

Average Order: $2,500

This is the average order amount from individual sales. In this example, the average order value is $2,500, but in most cases average order amounts can be much higher and this does not take into account the lifetime value of a new customer or client.

Website Design and Development Cost: $10,000

This budget is the one-time spend to develop a basic website structure and the foundation for online marketing action items. This can include design, technology, content, photography and all other costs needed to launch the website and social media sites. This does not include the ongoing web marketing work for content, website updates and other web marketing costs.

Monthly Web Marketing Spend: $3,000

This is the amount of money spent monthly to market and maintain the website and on other online marketing efforts, such as social media and AdWords. Traffic generation is an important part of this budget and should include staff time and external contractor hours.

Total Monthly Website Visitors: 2,000

This is the total number of monthly visits to your website. This number can be either total visits or unique visitors. It is best to generally monitor total visits or sessions as the key indicator. This is part of the ROI equation controlled by web marketers. Generally, the higher the targeted traffic, the greater number of leads for the sales team.

Conversion Rate to Leads: 2.5 percent (50 leads)

This is the conversion rate of online visitors to sales leads. The number of leads divided by the site's traffic equals your conversion rate. Keep in mind, there are many ways to convert website visitors into sales leads. The key factor here is that they have made contact with your company and are now in touch with your sales team. Target a conversion rate of 1 to 5 percent for lead generation websites. The better your website converts, the higher the amount of sales leads. This is an ROI factor you and the web marketing team can influence with excellent content and a high-performing website. Much of this book is really about maximizing this conversion rate.

Lead Conversion Rate to a Sale: 20 percent

This is a measurement of how successful your sales team is at converting a sales lead into a closed sale. If one out of every five sales leads converts into a sale, your conversion rate is 20 percent. Calculate this number by dividing the total number of sales orders by the total number of leads in that same time period. Most sales teams convert at higher than 20 percent and this is a conservative number for this ROI example. Sales teams with strong performance convert at 50 percent or higher, depending on the average order amount. For example, higher price points tend to convert at lower conversion rates.

10 Sales per Month = $25,000

This is the total number of monthly sales in gross dollars given the amount of sales generated by the sales team. Your average order amount times the number of sales equals gross sales volume. Remember, this represents gross sales and not profitability, which is a separate ROI formula based on how you manage and monitor expenses.

ROI FORMULA: Lead Generation Website

Here is the ROI formula for lead generation websites. Keep in mind this data is measuring gross sales or top line revenue. You may find other factors that are unique to your company to help calculate ROI and these numbers will change based on your costs and other factors.

Total Website Traffic x Online Conversion Rate x Average Order Amount x Lead Conversion Rate = Total Gross Sales.

— or —

Here is what the formula looks like when we put in the numbers from the example above.

(2,000 x 2.5 percent) x $2,000 x 20 percent = $25,000

Divide this number by your total spend to determine your ROI percentage.

You can see from this example, $3,000 per month in web marketing spend is producing $25,000 per month in gross sales.

ROI TRACKING: E-commerce Websites

The second ROI example is for e-commerce websites generating orders directly from an online store and shopping cart. Here are the key components of ROI calculations for e-commerce websites.

Average Order Amount: $150

This is the average order amount for individual orders placed on the e-commerce website. It includes groupings of various products and is a total order amount. Shipping costs should not be included in this number. E-commerce websites in general will need to produce healthy average order amounts to produce a solid ROI. Many e-commerce sites fail because the average order amount is too low and there is not enough traffic or sales to cover costs.

Website Design/Development Cost: $15,000

The total price of an e-commerce website is usually higher than the cost of a content-based, lead generation website and $15,000 is a good benchmark for basic e-commerce sites. Complex online shopping sites require higher budget amounts.

Monthly Web Marketing Spend: $4,000

This is the amount spent each month to market and maintain the website.

Total Monthly Website Visitors: 5,000

E-commerce websites survive on traffic generation and should work hard to grow website traffic, while maintaining conversion rates. This is the number of total monthly visits to the site.

Order Conversion Rate: 2 percent (100 sales)

Target a conversion rate of at least 2 percent. Some e-commerce websites have conversion rates as high as 15 percent or more. Seasonality also plays a big factor in conversion rates. For example, conversion rates increase substantially during holiday periods.

100 Sales per Month = $15,000

The website's conversion rate is a direct indicator of online sales success. E-commerce sites with higher conversion rates are more profitable. The number of sales times the average order amount equals total gross sales for the month.

ROI FORMULA: E-commerce Websites

Here is the ROI formula for e-commerce websites:

Total Website Traffic x Online Conversion Rate x Average Order Amount = Total Gross Sales.

- or -

Here is what the formula looks like when we put in the numbers from the e-commerce example above.

(5,000 x 2 percent) x $150 = $15,000

Divide this number by your total spend to determine your ROI percentage.

These calculations do not account for shipping and other factors that may impact conversion rates, average order amounts, and profitability.

SUMMARY

Once you have set goals and you are accurately tracking website data, the challenge becomes finding ways to better market online and improve your ROI. Those are the goals of this book and the benchmarks that define how you will win the website war! Go back and review each section to learn how to implement action plans that get results and improve ROI. Also, use the ROI worksheets in this chapter to determine your monthly ROI.

ACTION ITEMS

➤ Establish a web marketing ROI calculating worksheet that is unique to your company to determine ROI.

➤ Plug in your numbers and see what your potential ROI is from web marketing if you can improve traffic and conversion rates.

➤ Bring completed web marketing ROI worksheets to your next web marketing meeting for review and discussion.

➤ Learn more about web marketing to improve each part of the ROI formula.

➤ Develop action plans for each part of the ROI process and track your results.

PART THREE:
IMPLEMENTATION
& ACTION PLANS

CHAPTER 50

How to Develop and Assign Work to Your Web Marketing Team

I n part one of this book we introduced you to the Four-Step Process. In part two, we went into detail on each of the four steps. In part three, we will pull all the steps together with instructions on how to successfully implement the action plans needed to exceed your web marketing goals.

Let's start with the web marketing team. These are the people that will implement the Four-Step Process and make web marketing action plans reality. Each major job function or role has been broken down into eight distinct areas. As we mentioned previously, the position titles can change as needed, but the core functions remain the same for each position. In this chapter we will review the action items for each separate job function.

Web Marketing Team Action Items

We discussed the web marketing team in chapter 16. This chapter will look closer at the work assignments and action plans for each member of this team. Your job as the team leader will be to pull this team together, understand their roles and assign action items to the appropriate team member. Please review chapter 16 for an understanding of each person's role in web marketing. Here is a list of action items for each job function.

Internet Marketing Director/Manager

This is the web marketing lead responsible for the strategy and leading the entire web marketing process. Action items for this position deal with leadership, strategy and building a winning team to include the following:

- Researches and writes the web marketing plan
- Sets the strategy for web marketing efforts
- Ensures the strategy is being followed by the web marketing team
- Leads the web marketing meetings
- Suggests improvements to the strategy to improve results
- Reviews web marketing data weekly or monthly
- Asks questions of the web marketing team about results
- Evaluates the web marketing team's performance and their results
- Makes the final decisions on web marketing action items when necessary

Internet Project Manager/Coordinator

This position is so important we have devoted chapter 51 of this book solely to the project manager position. Many web marketing projects fail because of poor project management, or no project management whatsoever. It's best for this position to be internal to your company and not outsourced. Here is a summary of a few key action items in this critical position:

- Schedules and organizes the web marketing meetings
- Organizes and follows up on action plans
- Is the taskmaster for communication between the web marketing team members
- Updates online project management software for improved team coordination
- Looks for inconsistencies in team member action items
- Checks the website for broken links and other errors
- Prepares due dates for action items
- Helps recruit and replace team members as needed
- Communicates with contracted team members and other subcontractors
- Organizes website content timing and placement on the website and in social media

Internet Marketing Specialist

This position is responsible for driving traffic to the website, and will have some crossover with the action items for the website research specialist. This position may also be broken into several job functions based on the variety of skills and action items needed to drive traffic. This position may be internal to your company or outsourced depending on the necessary skill levels.

- Prepares and implements a traffic generation plan for the website and social media

- Conducts keyword research and the development of keyword themes

- Responsible for the development and placement of title tags and meta descriptions for all website pages and modifications as needed

- Provides search engine optimization (SEO) of website code and content

- Conducts on-page content review to drive SEO results by targeted keywords

- Set up, management and review of AdWords and all online advertising programs

- Management of the monthly e-mail newsletter and other e-mail marketing efforts

- Oversees and sets up all social media efforts for consistent design, content postings and distribution through the best social media outlets

- Works with the content writer on regular blog posting topics and SEO coding for all blog posts and other content pages

- Develops and requests links from websites visited by the target market to the company website, and oversees the link building programs for the website, both locally and globally, tracking results

- Makes sure offline marketing efforts are coordinated with online marketing and traffic generation, and tracks direct traffic from offline marketing efforts

- Reviews and prepares analysis of website traffic sources as seen in web stats

- Sets up and monitors Google Analytics and Webmaster Tools

- Prepares reports on conversion rates by traffic source

Website Research Specialist

Accurately tracking website data and the site's overall usability is the responsibility of this job position and may be combined with the Internet Marketing Specialist. Key tasks are focused on collecting data and research to improve results and reporting those findings to marketing and sales leadership.

- Reviews web stats weekly or monthly, comparing them against previous months/years, and spots trends in the data, making recommendations

- Develops user testing programs to gather feedback from website users

- Reviews stats and data from e-mail campaigns

- Sets up and reviews data and interactions from social media efforts

- Develops reports for the web marketing team and company leadership

- Researches and analyzes web marketing software and reports to constantly improve web marketing results

- Sets up tracking for all relevant website conversion points

Content Writer for the Web

This position is a dedicated writer of website content, to include service and product descriptions, website articles, blog postings, social media content and other forms of written web marketing content. This position can be internal or outsourced, depending on the amount of content needed.

- Meets with the web marketing team on a content plan that includes content topics, distribution channels and a schedule for generating written content

- Recommends content approaches for length of content and use of headers by content type

- Reviews web stats on the most popular content and how it is being read by website visitors and recommends new content topics

- Ensures all written content is in a format easily read and understood by online visitors

Photography and Other Media

This can be a team of people responsible for the website's media including photography, video, audio, podcasts, slide presentations

WINNING THE **WEBSITE WAR**

and other media. These team members follow direction from the web marketing team and are most likely outsourced contractors who are specialists in each area.

- Prepares photo shoots, captures the photos and edits them for online placement

- Prepares the story board and script for video production work

- Shoots, mixes the sound and edits online videos

- Records and edits audio recordings, such as podcasts, music and other audio clips

- Works with the graphic designer on layout and placement of all media elements

- Insures all media is easy to use on the website and provides value to visitors

Graphic Designer

This position is the site's graphic artist and is responsible for the website's overall graphics and design. The graphic designer's ongoing action items include several key areas.

- Prepares the home page and interior page designs

- Updates the home page rotator and graphics as needed

- Integrates the website's messaging and taglines into the graphics of the website

- Ensures all photos, videos and other graphic elements have the proper copyright for use on the Internet and that they look professional on the site

- Works with the technology team so graphic elements are properly added to the website and coded for SEO purposes

- Provides design elements for all social media sites and other online graphics

Technology Professional

The technology team converts graphic designs to website code, handles the site's hosting, is responsible for the website's technology platform and all other technical issues associated with online marketing efforts. This position is best outsourced.

- Selects the appropriate website platform that meets the needs of the website strategic plan and can also be edited by internal team members

- Establishes the hosting environment for the site, along with e-mail accounts

- Sets up access to the website's administrative sections with passwords and training for making website edits and updates

- Sets up and oversees the security functions for the website and other spam and malware protections

- Oversees the integration of the website with any company software modules such as accounting systems, CRM software, inventory or other types of software

- Other technical issues that impact the usability and success of the website

SUMMARY

Use these action item summaries to develop action plans for each team member. Remember to avoid giving action items to any team members without the skills and knowledge to do excellent work in their area of focus. Be cautious of team members who claim to have multiple skill sets, such as a technologist who is also a designer. It is best to build a team of specialists and provide clear direction based on your web marketing strategic plan. Keep in mind, the web marketing team will be a mix of internal and outsourced people. The effectiveness of the team is driven by excellent project management and by putting the right people in place to implement your web strategy.

WINNING THE **WEBSITE WAR**

ACTION ITEMS

➤ Develop your web marketing team and assign tasks to each person. Start with a project manager.

➤ Schedule time to meet with each team member to review their assigned action items and to build accountability for results.

➤ Determine who is needed in regular web marketing meetings.

➤ Schedule and run regular web marketing meetings to keep the team on track.

➤ Use the content in this book to write job descriptions, assign tasks to internal employees and to recruit contractors to build your web marketing team.

➤ Adjust budgets as needed based on web marketing ROI to determine which team members are internal to the company and which are outsourced as contractors.

TRUE STORY – Only the Names Have Been Changed to Protect Privacy

"Siri just recommended our website to a new patient! How does that happen?" asked George Adams, the owner of University Sports Therapy. It happens when a well-defined web strategy and an attractive website generates traffic through the Four-Step Process. Of course, it also helps when the company provides excellent sports therapy services to their patients.

When George first began improving his web marketing efforts with the Four-Step Process, George said that he would be happy if his clinic could grow to fifty patients per week. His goal soon was met and surpassed. Their sports health clinic now treats up to eighty patients per week.

The strategy was to have the best website in their market, loaded with content for prospective patients and giving them the ability to make appointments online. It does not matter how many website visitors come to the site, unless they make contact and book an appointment.

"Patients actually make a point of telling us the website was the best they experienced online in our community, and our patient growth is at a new high," continued George. "Our accountant actually called and asked what we were doing to have such an impact on revenues. My answer was quick—the Four-Step Process for web marketing. He told me we should have done that a long time ago."

Here is how George and his team implemented the four steps:

Strategy: They designed the best looking website in the local marketplace and allowed for interactions, such as online appointment setting for repeat patients. They also created excellent content on the site so that prospective patients could easily research the clinic.

Design and Development: The clinic backs up the website design with excellent content and a user-friendly website that makes it easy to connect with the company.

Traffic Generation: The site targets SEO niches and includes very focused AdWords campaigns with strong calls to action. They also provide excellent service so people keep coming back to the website for content and to book repeat appointments.

Monitoring ROI and Tracking Results: They closely track website traffic stats and the amount of new patients coming from web marketing efforts. They ask for feedback about how patients use the website so it can be improved over time.

The Results: The clinic is now at close-to-full capacity. This provides income for the owners, employees and excellent treatment for clinic patients.

CHAPTER 51

How to Develop Action Plans and Project Manage Web Marketing

In this chapter we will look at the role of the web marketing project manager in more detail. The project manager is one of the first people to add to the web marketing team and will be key to excellent results. The project manager is the glue that holds all the action items and team members together so that the web marketing strategy can be realized. Don't take this position lightly. This should be an internal position in the company and you must give them the tools and responsibility to properly project manage web marketing priorities.

Web Marketing Team Selection

It takes time to find the right people and build your web marketing team. Web marketers are in high demand and their skill sets and experience can vary greatly. The project manager plays an important roles in this area. He or she should be tasked with implementing the legwork and developing a process to find, interview and recruit web marketing team members. This includes both employees and contractors.

Because web marketing work is easily measured and results are very transparent, develop a test project for new team members to assess their work ethic, skills and job performance before they are hired. The project manager should cover the details needed to make this happen and help build the team. The project manager should also make recommendations regarding replacing poorly performing team members.

Web Marketing Meetings

A key job function for the project manager is the scheduling and organizing of web marketing meetings. He or she should help prepare the agenda, determine who needs to attend, and track the action items coming out of each meeting. Over time, the project manager may even run the meeting and keep team members on track. One of the most important outcomes from web marketing meetings will be action item assignments and due dates. These are managed and tracked by the project manager.

Reviewing Priorities and Measuring Results

The project manager may not have the final say on web marketing priorities and action plans, but should be involved in reviewing those areas and understanding how to measure results. This includes organizing and following up on action plans. Not all the action items are of equal importance, and the team can't do everything at once. This is where the project manager comes in to keep the action items prioritized by their impact on web marketing goals and implementing the web marketing strategy. It is important to keep the project manager aware of the big picture and the ROI of web marketing efforts.

Oversight of the Web Marketing Team

The project manager is the taskmaster for communication between each of the web marketing team members. This includes communications with contracted team members and other subcontractors as well as employees of the company. The project manager looks for inconsistencies in team member action items, and because the project manager has access to all the action items, this person is in a unique position to make sure things stay on track. This includes feedback on the performance of each team member.

Website Updates and Content Reviews

The project manager should also spot-check the work of the web marketing team. This includes checking the website for broken links and other technical and design glitches, along with other things, such as grammar and spelling errors. The project manager should also work with the team to organize the timing of website content and placement of content on the website and in social media.

SUMMARY

The web marketing project manager is a key position on the web marketing team. Without this position, website marketing projects can go haywire very easily. Lack of proper project management is a critical factor in the failure of many website design and development projects. This position manages action items and processes and does not necessarily supervise team members. The project manager can report on team member performance, but it is not this person's role to manage those individuals. Put in place a strong project manager as the key driver of the company's web marketing projects.

ACTION ITEMS

> Determine a project manager for the web marketing team.

> Provide the proper web-based project management software and communication tools needed for this person's success.

> Spend time reviewing projects and team member performance with the project manager outside of web marketing meetings.

> Share this book with the project manager to help him or her better understand the big picture and strategic nature of web marketing.

CHAPTER **52**

Web Marketing and the Sales Process

his final chapter is devoted to merging web marketing action items with the efforts of the sales team. This is absolutely critical to sales success because it is the sales team that usually closes sales and builds long-term relationships with clients and customers. Online marketing efforts will attract people to the company, and it is the sales team's job to close the sale and build the customer relationship. All this is part of the new sales funnel discussed in previous chapters.

In this chapter, we will cover how the Internet changed personal selling, how to transition a web conversion to the sales team so it can be closed, and how sharp, web-savvy salespeople may be the best individuals to include on the web marketing team. Let's start with how the Internet and web marketing have changed selling.

Selling and Marketing Turned Upside Down

The arrival of the Internet caused a selling revolution by putting a greater amount of purchasing and decision-making authority in the hands of prospective buyers, rather than sellers. If your website does not have what prospects want, another website will meet their needs. Today's sales force is no longer the company's primary source of new sales prospects for products and services. Prospects can now find your company online in great numbers, without first talking to a salesperson at your company. This has put an end to much of traditional sales prospecting, and has driven many lead generation efforts online.

As people strive to be more efficient with their time, prospects in your target market don't make time for meetings with sales reps to learn about products and services. In fact, sales managers and reps who have time for fact-finding meetings will not be at their jobs very long. Their focus should be on lead generation and attracting prospects to the company.

It is much faster and easier for people to research solutions on the web and make contact when they are ready to buy. Companies must adapt to this changing environment and realize ROI from cold calling, prospecting and sales meetings is quickly diminishing. This changing environment, driven by the web, has turned sales and marketing upside down and changed traditional sales roles in many ways.

Traditional Sales Roles Have Changed

Traditional selling models involved the basics of prospecting, qualifying, presenting, handling objections and closing. Old-school salespeople spent most of their time finding prospects they could meet and qualify. This process is becoming obsolete, and the roles have changed as the prospective customer and/or client is now in charge of prospecting and qualifying via web searches and online content. The online research of prospective customers has replaced many traditional sales activities!

In the majority of cases, the company website has become the first stop in the sales process. This is the vital first step of the sales process and in moving a prospect toward a sale.

In the past, prospects relied on the salesperson's knowledge and sales abilities to move toward a closed sale. This is no longer the case, as the Internet is the main resource for these buyers to learn, and they no longer have much time for cold calling salespeople. So what is the role of salespeople? Are they necessary? Absolutely!

With the exception of e-commerce websites, many sales leads generated by web marketing will involve contact with a company sales representative, or will be included in stay-in-touch programs. In addition, salespeople can be excellent at web marketing; more to come on that later in the chapter. The challenge is to extend the Four-Step Process of web marketing into the company's sales process and in training salespeople how to market online.

Web Leads and the Sales Strategy

It is important to develop a sales strategy and process for handling web leads and sales. The sales team must be trained in this process and there must be accountability for closing web leads. This is critical to web marketing ROI and a strong sales team should be able to close 25-50 percent of all web leads. Those that do not close should become part of the company's stay-in-touch program. The sales team should clearly understand how people become sales leads from web marketing strategies, and they should take these leads seriously. It is important to include sales management in the web marketing meetings on occasion, and explain how people use the company website and convert into sales leads. This will help the sales team better understand the online prospect and develop a strategy that will close more sales. It will also provide the web marketing team with valuable insights on how to convert more site visitors into leads.

Response Times and the Importance of a Web Lead

Extending your web marketing process into the sales process starts with recognizing the importance of a web lead. This should go without saying; however, many sales organizations still do not respond fast enough to web leads or recognize how important these leads are to closing sales. This should be a part of the sales team's culture and personality. This guidance will come from the sales and marketing leadership team.

People expect fast response times from salespeople, and if you don't do it, your competitors will. Web technologies allow for quick response time, and this has increased dramatically within successful selling teams. The sales team should respond to web leads immediately or within a few minutes. In fact, live chat and other web technologies allow salespeople to respond immediately to inquiries and other requests from prospects. This is the best way of showing just how important a web lead is to the company's growth. Salespeople can also play a role in lead generation and prospecting by contributing to the web marketing team.

Website visitors want fast response times, but they don't want to deal with intrusive salespeople. The sales team must find the right balance with live chat and other resources to maximize sales conversions.

Salespeople as Web Marketers

Salespeople can make great web marketers. This is true because they best understand the customer, and are on the front line of the customer relationship. Salespeople must be integrated into web marketing because web marketing is one of the primary drivers of sales leads and the sales process! It is critical to their success. Successful salespeople must know how to identify and connect with prospects from the world's best lead generator, the Internet.

Salespeople must learn the basics of online marketing to drive leads. Web leads and prospects are usually highly qualified leads. Prospecting, historically the most time consuming part of the old sales process, can be skipped in its entirety and the focus can be placed on generating leads from the web. The sales rep can move right into highly-qualified selling and closing with an educated prospect that has researched online.

Great Salespeople are Perfect for Web Marketing

A sales rep's value and the overall marketing ROI to your business will increase dramatically if salespeople can market online. The good news: the fundamentals of web marketing are similar to the basics of selling. Your company's website is now a key sales tool and needs to function like a great prospector and presenter of information. The website should be easy to use and simple to understand with a focus on key benefits. The site should push visitor hot buttons to drive inquiries. The best salespeople on your team should have an intuitive understanding of how to get this done. It is too expensive to pay for prospecting efforts when those efforts produce such poor ROI. Businesses that take a web-savvy approach to selling will outpace competitors, and the changing role of the company sales rep can make an impact.

The Role of Salespeople in Web Marketing Starts with Education

If salespeople are to make the transition from traditional sales roles to web marketers, they must first learn the basics of web marketing. This is a personal choice and if they are not willing to learn there is not much hope. The necessary skills will not come from a college or university. Internet marketing skills are developed by doing, watching and acting on results. It is critical to stay on top of changes, which can literally happen overnight.

Also, there is no quick fix! It takes time and effort to get web marketing efforts optimized and successful. This effort will pay off many times over with increased leads and sales. Anyone can learn these skills at a minimal cost from many free resources available online and from the content in this book. The biggest challenge is finding the salespeople with the desire and motivation to make the change and learn a new approach to sales. Let's take a look at the specific skills needed by salespeople to become effective web marketers.

What Web Marketing Skills are Needed? Follow the Four Steps:

Salespeople do not have to be IT or design professionals to be successful at web marketing. The key is to provide strategic, sales-focused direction to IT and design professionals. This process will not be successful unless the sales team has a basic understanding of the Internet marketing strategy for the company. To gain this understanding, salespeople should start with the basics. They first need to learn about the four steps:

- Strategy

- Design and Development

- Driving Traffic

- Website Performance

These four steps are the foundation for salespeople learning about web marketing and developing an action plans to drive results.

Salespeople and Online Content Distribution

Each of the four steps leads to a lengthy list of action items. Once the website has an excellent strategy and great design, the next step is driving traffic. The salesperson's role in driving traffic is mostly based on written content. In fact, content preparation for the website and social media may be the most common tasks performed by salespeople in their roles as web marketers. This content can be posted on the company website and blog, written in articles, used in e-mail marketing or throughout the Internet on a variety of websites. Salespeople should be able to write excellent customer-focused content.

Content preparation is the most time consuming, yet most effective role of a web marketer. Website content comes in a variety of formats and here are a few examples of content types perfect for sales professionals:

- E-mail newsletters

- Blog postings

- Podcasts

- Webinars

- Informational articles

- Social media postings

- Product and services descriptions

This is how salespeople must sell today, and in the future. The traditional sales pitch has been replaced by carefully crafted, inviting websites, informative e-mail contacts and effective use of social media content and resources. Salespeople must become experts on their product and services, facilitate expert discussions, tell stories and understand in great depth how targeted markets use the Internet.

How to Find and Train Salespeople to Market Online

Hiring is the greatest challenge in developing an effective web marketing and/or sales team. Finding a sales rep with online marketing skills, or the desire to learn those skills, makes hiring an even greater challenge. However, finding a salesperson with those skills is a real benefit to the company and to the salesperson. The organization gets more sales and leads, and the sales rep gets more enjoyment from the work. The challenges are to find salespeople with those skills or find ways to convert current sales team members into web marketers by providing access to online marketing job functions or web marketing training. It's difficult to do, but not impossible.

Hiring and Training Recommendations

Here are a few suggestions for hiring and training salespeople to market online.

- Look for salespeople that are very comfortable on the web and are good at writing content. People that have attempted to build a website or frequently use Facebook and other social media sites are good candidates, and will naturally want to learn more about web marketing and look forward to posting content.

- These salespeople should have a high comfort level with technology, and a passion for the Internet and web marketing knowledge. Without this passion, there may be little incentive to learn and practice online marketing skills.

- Encourage learning about web marketing from proven web resources. You can find nearly unlimited resources online. Make the time for salespeople to try out what they learn and convert natural selling skills to web marketing. Set up web stats and ROI tracking to measure their performance.

- It is important to modify incentive and rewards systems around web marketing skills that include lead creation, online conversions, an understanding of web stats, e-mail marketing and more.

Some of the best candidates for web marketing positions may already be a part of your current sales team. Investigate internally to find skills that go beyond traditional selling and into a more effective web marketing approach to drive leads. Watch out for non-technical salespeople, because they will find it more difficult over time to generate leads and close sales; although, non-technical salespeople may have excellent writing skills.

Follow-Up and Stay-in-Touch Programs for Web-Based Sales

Web marketing is tremendously powerful to not only create sales leads, but also to cost-effectively stay in touch with a large universe of potential customers at a very low cost. However, the best lead generation in the world is meaningless unless salespeople are prepared to make multiple contacts with their prospects. In this way, salespeople are a major factor in successful stay-in-touch programs as part of their sales process. Get the sales team involved in e-mail blasts, online content and other stay-in-touch programs.

Most Salespeople Give Up Too Early

Research with salespeople has shown sales prospects need multiple contacts before they are ready to buy. Most salespeople fail because they do not communicate enough with prospects until they are ready to buy. Salespeople often give up because of assumptions they make about prospects and the amount of work needed to close a sale. It is not enough to train salespeople to generate leads from the web without also learning how to cost- effectively keep in touch until the sale is closed.

Stay-in-Touch Methods

As we discussed in previous chapters, staying in touch with prospects revolves around online content. Content serves the dual purpose of driving traffic and keeping in touch with your target market. The major rule of thumb is the content must be relevant and of high interest to the prospect, or it will be ignored. Content must either improve the quality of life or help people do their jobs more effectively. Also, all content should end up on the company blog or website. Here are examples of how salespeople can use content for stay-in-touch programs with web leads.

- **E-mail Newsletters** – Collect e-mail names/addresses and send monthly newsletters.

- **Webinars** – Develop a free 45-minute webinar to present quarterly.

- **Podcasts** – Reach a massive audience for free on iTunes with ten-minute audio segments.

- **Blogs** – Keep a running journal of value-added content that informs and tells a story.

- **Website Content Updates** – Develop a process of regular updates to your website.

- **Facebook, LinkedIn and Twitter** – Communicate small nuggets of information and build discussions on all major social media sites.

CRM and Google Analytics

CRM tools such as SaleForce.com can help track content used in stay-in-touch programs and provide data on prospect responses. Google Analytics reports on which content is most popular, and provides a wealth of information on the results of content distribution strategies. Also, search engines love content. These strategies will not only help you keep in touch with prospects, but also improve your organic search engine rankings. The goal is to focus on automation and reaching a maximum number of people with content they want to read and share with others. This is part of the sales process, and your sales team will play an important role in writing and distributing this content to the right prospects.

SUMMARY

The Internet has proved to be the best lead generator in history. It has become both the local and global Yellow Pages, replacing the phone book and providing unlimited information about your products and services to prospective customers, without excessive fees. This chapter has made the case that successful salespeople must learn to create qualified leads from web marketing efforts. The sales team may be the business leader's best resource for building a winning web marketing team to win the website war!

ACTION ITEMS

> Develop a list of web marketing resources for training salespeople.

> Provide the sales team with web marketing learning resources.

> Interview the sales team for web interests, skills and passion.

> Identify salespeople that should run web marketing programs.

> Assign content and follow-up responsibilities to members of the sales team.

> Include the sales process or funnel in your web marketing plan.

> Train the sales team on how to best handle web leads.

> Integrate the web marketing process with the sales process through the company CRM.

> Involve key salespeople in the company's web marketing processes.

> Give this book to sales managers and to each member of your sales team!

Conclusion

Business leaders are in a unique position to translate what their company does very well to the world's most important communication channel, the Internet. They need a clear understanding of how to do that and an excellent web marketing team to make it happen. These are the two most important keys to success in winning the website war. This book has outlined a process, strategies and action plans to make that happen and help you win at web marketing.

One of the major benefits of this book is to see web marketing from a new perspective and as a process to be worked and monitored. As your sales and marketing teams strive to increase sales they are looking for competitive advantages and unique techniques to reach their goals. The Four-Step Process will help provide direction needed to accomplish those goals. This book is a competitive advantage for those companies choosing to follow the four steps and find ways to rise above the competition.

I hope you have enjoyed this book and will take action on the strategies presented in these pages and through our online resources. Good luck in your web marketing efforts, and I wish you great success in winning the website war!

Online Resources

There are too many online tools and resources to mention in this book. We reviewed hundreds of websites and online tools and have summarized a few of the most important for the business leader. Many of these resources will contain links to many more tools to be evaluated as a possible fit for your business.

Essential Tools and Resources from Google

Google is the starting point for the most essential web marketing tools and resources. Google has a variety of web tools that are standards in web marketing and statistics. They are also free. These tools can be found by searching Google and developing an account with Google under one user name and password. Make sure you keep those Google login credentials in a safe place and that they always stay with the company.

You will find these resources discussed throughout this book. Here are a few of the most important Google tools:

- Google Analytics
- Google Keyword Tool (Found in AdWords)
- Google Webmaster Tools
- Google AdWords
- Google Alerts
- Google Insights for Search
- Google Think Insights

Website Strategy Resources

- Internet Marketing Plan Outline
- Website Review Checklist
- The Business Leader's Web Marketing Action Plan
- IntuitiveWebsites.com
- IntuitiveWebsites.com/4-Step-Process
- Hubspot.com
- Shop.org

Website Design and Development Tools

- WordPress.org
- MagentoEcommerce.com
- WhichTestWon.com
- UserTesting.com
- BuiltWith.com

SEO (Search Engine Optimization) Tools and Resources

- SearchEngineLand.com
- SearchEngineWatch.com
- AdvancedWebRanking.com
- MOZ.com
- Google Keyword Tool in AdWords
- WordTracker.com

PPC (Pay-per-Click) Resources

- Google Adwords
- WordStream.com
- MSN - BingAds.com

Must-Have Social Media Websites

- Facebook.com
- LinkedIn.com
- YouTube.com
- Twitter.com
- Google+
- Pinterest.com

Social Media Tools and Resources

- SocialMediaExaminer.com
- Google Alerts
- SocialMention.com
- HootSuite.com

E-mail Marketing Tools

- MailChimp
- iContact
- Constant Contact

Content Marketing Resources

- Checklist of Content Marketing Types
- Checklist of Content Marketing Channels
- Content Marketing Packet
- ContentMarketingInstitute.com

Online PR Resources

- PRWeb.com
- PR.com
- PRNewswire.com

Website Stats and ROI Resources

- Sales Lead ROI Worksheet
- Online Sale ROI Worksheet
- ROI Calculator for Online Conversions (link to IW calculator)
- LeadLander.com
- Google Analytics
- Alexa.com
- BuiltWith.com

Books

Don't Make Me Think by Steve Krug

SPIN Selling by Neil Rackham

ROI Worksheet: Online Sales Lead

Here is a sample ROI worksheet for determining your return from online sales leads as a result of web marketing efforts.

Marketing ROI Worksheet for Lead Generation

Time Frame: _____
(The time frame is the amount of time for the ROI calculations. Monthly time frames are common.)

Total Online Visits: _____

Conversion Rate to Leads: (Target a 2-5% conversion rate) _____

Total Online Leads: _____

Conversion Rate to Sales: (Target 30% or more) _____
(This is the conversion rate measurement for your sales team converting sales leads into closed business.)

Number of Orders: _____

Average Order Amount: _____

Total Sales: _____

Web Marketing Spend: _____

ROI: (Marketing Spend/Total Sales) _____

Cost per Customer Acquisition: _____

ROI Worksheet: E-commerce Sale

Here is a sample ROI worksheet for determining return on direct online sales from an e-commerce website.

Marketing ROI Worksheet for Direct Online Ecommerce Sale

Time Frame: _____
(The time frame is the amount of time for the ROI calculations. Monthly time frames are common.)

Total Website Visits: _____

Conversion Rate to Orders: (Target a 3-5% conversion rate) _____

Number of Orders: _____

Average Order Amount: _____
(Target an average order amount of at least $75 for eCommerce sales.)

Total Sales: _____

Marketing Spend: _____

ROI: (Marketing Spend/Total Sales) _____

Cost per Customer Acquisition: _____

Author's Biography

Thomas Young is a business owner, consultant, speaker and author. He is President and Owner of Intuitive Websites, LLC, a Colorado-based website design, development and marketing firm. His company merges marketing and technology to help companies of all sizes create and market effective websites.

Tom has been a Vistage speaker since 2001, is a Vistage member, and part of the team that recently re-designed the Vistage Village website. He has twenty-five years of experience in marketing and sales, including Internet marketing and website usability research, and has helped hundreds of companies increase their sales through his consulting and web marketing work. He is passionate about understanding how people use the Internet and helping his clients succeed online.

He has presented around the U.S. and Canada on Internet marketing and web usability, and is the author of Intuitive Selling. Tom has a BA in communications from the University of Northern Colorado and an MBA from the University of Colorado. He is the father of two sons, an avid tennis player and musician. Visit IntuitiveWebsites.com to learn more.

Contact Information:

Thomas Young
1720 Jet Stream Drive #208
Colorado Springs, CO 80921
719-481-4040
tom@intuitivewebsites.com

Made in the USA
San Bernardino, CA
04 April 2018